MARRIAGE, DIVORCE
AND
FAMILY
JUSTICE

Policy Monographs 25

For Yon

Social Welfare Research Program

MARRIAGE, DIVORCE AND FAMILY JUSTICE

BARRY MALEY

THE CENTRE FOR
INDEPENDENT
STUDIES
1992

Barry Maley

Published January 1993 by

The Centre for Independent Studies Limited

National Library of Australia

Cataloguing-in-Publication Data:

Maley, Barry, 1925–
Marriage, divorce and family justice.

ISBN 0 949769 84 3.

[1.] Family law – Australia. 2. Divorce – Law and legislation – Australia. 3. Family policy – Australia.
I. Centre for Independent Studies (Australia).
II. Title. (Series : CIS policy monographs ; 25).

346.94015

Printed by Australian Print Group

Contents

Foreword

Few subjects of public debate are more important than the family. Few are so poorly debated. We all tend to have pet opinions on the subject and pet solutions for its ills. In private life that is mostly fine, for there we can each follow our own convictions. But in the public-policy arena diversity presents difficulties, for we must find common ground if we are to act together on matters affecting the well-being of the family.

How is such common ground to be found? We need to respect the diversity of people's preferences and practices. Yet we need also to affirm the value and importance of the family, so that its legitimate claims are not eroded and its status is not thoughtlessly undermined.

One way to approach this problem is to focus on the social significance of children. Barry Maley takes this path in part of *Marriage, Divorce and Family Justice*. (It was also the route which I took in much of my *The Family in the Welfare State*). The point of this approach is not to make partisan claims about how many or how few children 'we' should have, or about how much 'we' should value the next generation. Rather, its aim is to see that children are not valued and supported less than other relevantly similar members of the community (such as the elderly). This approach also tries to ensure that all children are given fair consideration, so that social support is not distributed selectively to some children but not to relevantly similar other children.

A very different approach to finding common ground on family policy is through the notion of marriage. How can marriage provide this when it is itself the subject of controversy and dissension? It is Maley's view, however, that we can discern common ground once we make a distinction between different kinds of marriage-like relationships. We can then devise policies that do justice to the diversity of people's commitments. In this way the claims of liberality and fairness can be reconciled.

To take this view is to take a stand on the content of these relationships. This Maley does. In his account marriage is, at least in part, a form of mutual commitment or contract. (If this seems obvious then we do at least have this much common ground.) It follows that the morality of marriage is, again at least in part, the morality of mutual commitments. And it follows also that, all else being equal, the law of marriage must take this fact about marriage into account.

Not every marriage-like relationship has the force and significance of marriage. Some couples do not want what marriage has to offer. In addition, some marriage partners choose to dissolve their relationship. Some spouses uphold their commitments; some break them. Since the 1970s Australian public policy has attempted to be 'neutral' about matters of this sort. But such neutrality is not at all the same as fairness; rather, it is an attempt to turn a blind eye to distinctions that are relevant and important. This kind of neutrality can be sustained only with the help of much double-think and obscurantism, which partly explains why public debate about the family is so difficult.

The strangest aspect of debate about the family is how rare it is to see basic principles stated and defended. The field is dominated by people, both theorists and practitioners, who seem to give not a moment's thought to the possibility of welfare dependency, to the dangers of state intrusiveness or to the integrity and autonomy of intact families. Maley's study is important because it states and defends principles that take these into account.

Marriage, Divorce and Family Justice is, as Maley puts it, 'an essay in finding principles in terms of which progress in sorting out particular questions might be made'. It is refreshingly free from weasel words and evasiveness. How can the mutual commitments of marriage be recognised in family law? Should spouses who are injured by the marriage-breaking actions of their former partners be entitled to damages in their divorce settlements? On broader social issues: Should two-parent families be compelled to support the children of couples who separate? Should parents who care for their children at home be required to subsidise families who use commercial or public childcare? These are some of Maley's uncomfortable questions.

The principles Maley espouses are widely supported, in my opinion. I also think he is exactly right when he says that 'A sound family policy is almost the whole of a good welfare policy'. How in detail a 'sound family policy' is to be constructed is still a matter for much consideration, but this contribution to the CIS Social Welfare Research Program is one valuable source of guidance for those of us interested in both families and justice.

Alan Tapper

Preface and Acknowledgements

Marriage and family life are subjects impossible to deal with comprehensively in a single volume and least of all in a relatively short book such as this. It therefore confines itself to those topics judged to be central to dealing with some of the fundamental problems of contemporary marriage and family life. If it serves to help in understanding some of the sources of the unease about marriage and family that appears to be widespread in Australia today, it will have served its purpose. And the more so if it stimulates the public debate and reform that are long overdue.

The book in its present form has been greatly helped by the comments and suggestions of referees and by the editorial assistance of Michael James, Editorial Director of the Centre for Independent Studies, and by Andrew Davies, its Production Editor. Geoffrey Hogbin, Susan Bastick, James Cox and John Logan have helped refine some sections of the original manuscript with their comments, but any remaining deficiencies are, of course, entirely due to the author. As always, Greg Lindsay, Executive Director of the CIS, has been a source of patient and unfailing support.

About the Author

Barry Maley was educated at the University of Sydney and the Australian National University. He has been Senior Fellow at the Centre for Independent Studies since 1989. From 1971 to 1988 he was Senior Lecturer in the Faculty of Commerce at the University of New South Wales and during that period he studied also at the Universities of Oxford and Cambridge and the University of California at Los Angeles. His work with the CIS has ranged over various aspects of public policy, including education and training policy, entrepreneurship, 'industrial democracy' and welfare policy — particularly as it affects family structure and well-being. In addition to a variety of published work produced while at the University of New South Wales, he has contributed several articles to *Policy* and other CIS publications, together with many feature articles on public-policy issues in the daily press.

Executive Summary

1. Successful marriages and the well-being of families depend importantly upon just and predictable marriage law, the availability of work, and fair and modest taxation.

2. Family law in Australia fails to acknowledge and support the institutional character of marriage as a voluntary union and contract intended to be permanent.

3. Divorce must continue to be an available right, either consensually or by unilateral petition, without being conditional upon proof of 'fault'. But, since marriage is at least a contract, there should be provision for the issue of penalties/compensation for proven breach of the marital contract (e.g. cruelty, desertion, adultery, habitual intoxication, etc.) to be raised at the divorce **settlement**.

4. The Family Law Act 1975 allows too much judicial discretion, makes family law uncertain and unpredictable, encourages unreasonable litigation, raises costs and makes the delivery of marital justice problematic. There is scope for clarification, firm rules and greater certainty in the key areas of property, custody and maintenance.

5. Reform of family law by recognising the true character of marriage and by providing compensation for breach of marital contract would be just, would encourage more responsible and considered behaviour and would promote greater family stability.

6. Given a reformed legal basis for marital and family life, the availability of work for the able-bodied and modest taxation of families are essential for successful family formation, the development of 'human capital' and freedom from dependency on state welfare.

7. These conditions are not being met because:

    (i) protectionist policies, in combination with centralised labour market regulation, have entrenched high unemployment of the unskilled and poorly educated, creating the need for state welfare support;

(ii) the expansion of welfare support in other directions, particularly for sole parents and the aged, combined with many years of inflation and 'bracket creep', have imposed high levels of taxation on families, particularly single-income families with dependent children.

8. Divorce and family breakdown are occurring more frequently. The consequences — sole parenthood, higher proportions of ex-nuptial births, evasion of family maintenance responsibilities by former partners, and thus demands for state support — have led to behavioural and social problems among children separated from their biological parents and have increased the taxation burden on parents who stay together.

9. There is a strong argument, based upon the citizenship and 'taxpayer' status of children, for special treatment, by way of tax concessions or benefits, for the parents of dependent children.

10. Government out-of-home child-care policies are grossly unfair, inefficient, expensive, and deliberately directed, without sound social or economic justification, towards driving both parents into the workforce. The systems already established are becoming over-regulated and in process of capture by special-interest groups.

11. Greater justice for families with dependent children and enhanced family stability at reduced cost to federal revenue can be achieved by:

    (i) introducing a single, universal instrument for child-rearing and child-caring assistance in the form of a 'child tax credit/benefit' worth $2000 per annum for each child under age 16, to be used entirely at the discretion of the parents, and by abolishing all other forms of federal assistance for families, sole parents and out-of-home child care, and the dependent-spouse rebate;

    (ii) considering the further option of income-splitting for married couples with dependent pre-school children.

Chapter 1

Introduction

No human association or institution is more intimately crucial to what we are and what we will become than our own families. None is so fundamental in determining the endowments — physical, material, emotional and cultural — that shape our lives and the parts we play in our societies. It is the greatest of boons to be fortunate enough to be born into a good family; and one of the best things we can do with our own lives is to help create a good family ourselves.

The extent to which those good things happen depends to a large extent upon the initial health and strength of the family institution itself, upon the way in which the law supports it, and upon the economic and cultural vigour of other institutions. Men and women will do the rest spontaneously if they are given the opportunity to work together in their own ways under liberty and justice. What that means, concretely, is the subject of this study. But, for most of us, it all begins with marriage, and that is where we start.

Marriage: The Neglected Institution

Getting married is one of the great pivotal events in the lives of eight out of ten or so Australians. A happy marriage is one of life's gifts; a broken marriage, for most, one of its disasters.

So much hangs upon marriage for so many people that it is surprising how little consideration has been given to marriage as an **institution**; that is, as a public, law-governed system for ordering this most central of human relationships, and especially at a time when the institution has been undergoing radical changes. Much is said and written about **married life**, about the intimate and daily relationships between husbands and wives; indeed, as one aspect of our keen interest in people, such discussion never flags and plays a regular part in the daily fare of television, newspapers and magazines. But not much serious attention is devoted, even in the better newspapers and magazines, to marital law, the ways in which it has been changed, and the effects of these changes on marriage and divorce. This is doubly surprising in view of the considerable interest in divorce and divorce statistics, which, as most people are aware, have shown the increasing frequency of marriage breakdown over the last 15 years or so.

No doubt because of the publicity given to divorce figures, and complaints about the operations of the Family Court, political attention has been focused recently on the Family Law Act. As these words are being written, the enquiry of the Federal Parliamentary Joint Select Committee on Certain Aspects of the Operation and Interpretation of the Family Law Act is drawing to a close. This enquiry was given limited terms of reference that excluded discussion of what I believe to be some of the central shortcomings of the Family Law Act. Nevertheless, whatever its recommendations might be, they are likely to stimulate an overdue debate not only on the machinery of divorce, but also on the relation between marital breakdown and the legal framework of marriage.

This study consists largely of a re-examination of the nature of marriage and its legal environment. This necessarily includes an examination of the conditions under which marriages are dissolved by divorce. It argues that both the right to marry — in a sense decisively different from the 'right' to cohabit — and the right to divorce are profoundly important to the liberty of individuals and the welfare of families. In a just and well-ordered society, those rights are fundamental for men and women who **want** to marry and for those men and women who, perhaps finding their lives together intolerable, want to have the right, through divorce, to salvage an opportunity for a new life.

Delivering Justice

But rights carry obligations, especially the obligation not to crush the rights and legitimate expectations of others in exercising our own. The function of the state in a system of justice, no less in marriage than in other relations between citizens, is to maintain that balance. When the balance is right, good things follow; or, perhaps more accurately, are encouraged to follow. One of the goods so facilitated (but not guaranteed) is a greater scope for successful marriages, happy families and individual well-being.

Accordingly, a major part of our discussion is concerned with the issue of justice in marriage and divorce and with the task of finding the right balance between rights and obligations. It is not intended to be a definitive discussion of marriage and divorce — in any case impossible in a small volume like this — but rather an essay in finding **principles** in terms of which progress in sorting out particular questions might be made.

The discussion of marriage and divorce is important for its own sake, even when the issues are confined to husbands and wives. But much more is put at stake when children, too, are involved. The effective raising and care of children cannot be considered in isolation from the conditions, legal and otherwise, under which married life is conducted. If those conditions make married and family life more problematic than they need be, the integrity of families and the welfare of children are threatened.

Family Autonomy

In speaking of the 'integrity' of family life, I intend to give that term a particular meaning that will be made clearer in the main text. It suffices to say here that the term refers primarily to the autonomy and privacy of families as voluntary associations and to their capacity to acquire their own resources and to manage their own affairs.

Some students of the family, with the best of motives, put great emphasis on 'family stability' as a desirable objective, and they approach questions of marriage and divorce and the care of children with that objective in mind. Accordingly, they maintain that if divorce is made more difficult, for example, families will be made more stable and children will be raised in a more secure environment. This study, however, does not proceed from the assumption that family stability is necessarily a desirable end in itself, if by that is meant simply the formal continuation of the married state and of particular families as intact entities. The focus on stability may lead such thinkers to ignore (or insufficiently to examine) what is happening in the family, what **kind** of life it is living, and the moral and emotional states of its members. What is important is the nature of the bonds that hold a family together and of the forces that break it up. These should be the focus of interest. If internal solidarity arises spontaneously from the fulfilment of the members in their being together, that is good. But if stability is merely an 'external' fact arising wholly from the sheer physical or legal impossibility of living separately, then stability may be no more than a mask for misery. If family breakdown is caused by varieties of injustice, or by conflicting incentives acting upon its members, or by failure to live up to obligations enjoined by rights, then concern over those sources of instability and attention to them is certainly justified. The core of our argument in these matters is that delivery of justice in marriage and divorce is the prime function of family law. If it does that, we can then leave it to men and women, independently and privately, to find their own best arrangements, to define and seek their own stability, within the 'thickets of the law'.

In my opinion, the foundations of a successful way of life for the average family are autonomy, work, a framework of clear, certain and just law, and fair and modest taxation. This is the view that provides the framework for the discussion here of marriage, divorce, the care of children and family welfare in general. It is also, I maintain, important to keep these basic prerequisites in mind when considering family life in the context of the modern welfare state.

The Family and Social Welfare

Very few Australians would disagree with the proposition that, as a nation, we have a collective responsibility to provide a refuge of last resort for those who cannot provide for themselves or confidently depend upon relatives or other private individuals or organisations to help them. This is the 'safety net' view of the welfare state. In recent years, the taxation burden of the welfare state, and the seeming persistence of welfare problems despite very large state expenditures, has prompted rethinking of the respective welfare roles of the state and private initiatives. This rethinking has brought recognition of the crucial role that strong families play in delivering welfare. In a contribution to the CIS Social Welfare Research Program, James Cox (1992:14) concludes that 'the benefits that families provide for their members are clearly more valuable than government transfers'. To which we might add that the **absence** of strong families, for whatever reasons, itself enlarges the need for welfare services from other sources. If it is true, then, that social welfare is largely coextensive with the welfare of families, a national social-welfare policy that pays little attention to the conditions under which men and women voluntarily come together to begin families, prefer to stay together, enjoy having children and look after them well, is a bad welfare policy. A sound **family** policy is almost the whole of a good **welfare** policy.

The family is the one private, voluntary association to which all, at one time, belong. In its traditional form of married couple and children, it is a voluntary association that some 80 per cent or more of adults will establish and nurture to serve themselves, their children and often more distant relatives. In such an enterprise, the character of marriage, the circumstances of divorce, the incomes of families and the conditions under which children are born and raised are of the utmost importance. If we can get all of this right, or close to right, the enterprise will prosper and everyone will benefit. Trying to do so should be the single, greatest focus of the national will. This study is dedicated to helping realise that purpose.

4

The Organisation of This Study

The subjects to be discussed fall naturally into two parts. In Part One, the focus is primarily upon the nature of marriage, the relationships between law and marriage, the circumstances of divorce, and the need to rethink and reform family law. I believe that such an examination is an essential preliminary to understanding the present status of the Australian family in the wider social and economic context — a context dominated by the presence of a formidable welfare state and serious economic problems. It is these latter issues which form the substance of Part Two of the work. There, we analyse the ways in which welfare and economic policies (especially labour-market policies) are interacting to undermine the well-being of families by denying access to work, by encouraging dependency on the state and by over-taxing families with dependent children. These inequities are compounded by state child-care policies that are expensive, biased against family choice and in the process of being captured by special interests. Part Two concludes with some proposals for welfare benefit and taxation reforms intended to address the problems identified.

Chapter 2 is an 'orientating' chapter consisting largely of miscellaneous facts and statistics about marriage and family life in Australia. It is intended to give the non-specialist reader a bird's-eye view of a variety of information on these matters that is otherwise not easily available. The knowledgeable reader, or the reader who wants to go straight to the main substance of the work, may prefer to begin with chapter 3, on 'Justice in Marriage and Divorce'.

PART ONE

Marriage
and
Divorce

Chapter 2

The Present Condition of
Marriage and the Family

A s the French aphorism has it, 'the more things change, the more they remain the same'. Profound changes have occurred in marriage and family life in the last generation, and to assess their importance and implications for the future will be one of our main concerns. Yet men and women still get married, have children and try to raise them as best they can in a world that seems less sympathetic to that enterprise than it used to be. At the deepest levels, the levels of male-female pairing and the urge to form a family, much 'remains the same'. The family, as a universal human phenomenon, is resourceful and resilient in the face of hardship, oppression and ideological onslaughts. It has survived neglect and resisted dismemberment and persecution from a variety of tyrannies. It is, in these senses, the 'subversive family' of which Mount (1982) speaks and will remain the locus for the expression of the most permanent of human aspirations. But a rational and lively society must always attend to its institutions, listen to their heartbeats and then decide what, if anything, needs to be done.

As a prelude and background to what follows, a few basic facts and figures are given below to provide a quick thumbnail sketch of the dimensions of change — as well as the persistence of the perennial — in marriage and family matters.

Marriage is Popular; but So is Divorce

- Data from The Australian Institute of Family Studies' 1981–82 Australian Family Formation Survey (McDonald, 1983; Carmichael, 1986) indicate that about 80 per cent of people between the ages of 18 and 34 agreed that 'marriage is for life'; but 90 per cent also agreed that 'a couple should be able to get a divorce if they wanted to'.

- About eight out of ten men and women get married, but they are marrying much later and the proportion who will never marry is increasing.

- In 1971, of women aged 20, just on one in three was married. By 1986 only one in twelve 20-year olds was married (McDonald, 1988).

- The postwar marriage and baby boom came to an end in the early 1970s. That boom was an aberration from the later marriages and lower marriage rates of the late 19th and early 20th centuries. Why those earlier trends are reappearing — with the notable exception of earlier fertility levels — is one of the more interesting questions of the day.

- There are about 120 000 first marriages each year.

- There were 45 630 divorces in 1991, an increase of 7 per cent over 1990. The divorce rate has more than tripled over the last 30 years. One in three marriages will end in divorce. On average, such marriages last about ten years, although separation prior to divorce occurs after about seven or eight years (ABS, 1989c, 1992b).

- Most divorcees re-marry, but the divorce rate for second marriages is higher than for first marriages.

- There were 46 697 dependent children of people who were divorced in 1991. One in six 18-year olds will have seen their parents divorce.

- In 1991, 48.3 per cent of divorce applicants were wives and 36 per cent were husbands. The remaining 15.7 per cent were joint applications (ABS, 1992b).

- Divorce is more common among young couples without children (ABS, 1992b).

Cohabitation and De Facto Marriage Relationships

- If marriage and divorce are popular, so is cohabitation. Some 50 per cent of Australians under the age of 40 will cohabit at least once (*The Sydney Morning Herald*, 1991a).

- An Institute of Family Studies survey of people aged 18–34, carried out in 1985, showed that 8 per cent of men (but only 5 per cent of women) declared that they were living in a de facto marriage relationship, and that 18 per cent of men and 17 per cent of women had lived in such a relationship at some time.

- At the 1986 Census, 205 000 couples, or 6 per cent of all couple-families, were living in de facto marriage relationships.

- The rate of breakdown for de facto marriages is higher than for formal marriages.

Families and Children

There is some disagreement nowadays about the definition of 'family'., but for our purposes we intend the word to refer in most cases to parents and their children. However, in the following statistics the Australian Bureau of Statistics includes married couples with or without children, and other relatives.

- At June 1991, of the 4 502 000 families in Australia, there were 3 849 200 married-couple families, 383 500 single-parent families, and 269 400 'other families'. Of the single-parent families, 87 per cent had a female head (ABS, 1991a).

- The majority of families include dependent children. At June 1990, there were an estimated four million children between 0–15 years of age (ABS, 1991b).

- Contrary to claims sometimes made that the 'nuclear' or 'traditional' family is fast disappearing, and despite the rapid growth in sole-parent families, the overwhelming majority of dependent children still live in homes with two parents (ABS, 1991a).

- The Institute of Family Studies reports that 71 per cent of workers nominate 'family' as the source of their 'greatest satisfaction in life' (Institute of Public Affairs, 1987:10).

Mothers, Wives and Work

- At June 1991, in the 3 849 200 married-couple families in Australia, 1 017 700 wives (26 per cent) were working full time. Of these, just over half (538 200 or 52.8 per cent) had no dependants. Thus, about 12 per cent of mothers with dependants, in two-parent families, work full time (ABS, 1991a). This falls to about 4 per cent for mothers with two young children (Evans, 1988). Of the 922 100 wives who work part time, 636 000 have one or more dependants (ABS, 1991a).

- In the 335 200 female-headed, sole-parent families, 82 200 mothers were in full-time work, 64 300 in part-time work, 23 800 were unemployed, and 164 900 were not in the labour force (ABS, 1991b).

Fertility

- A fraction over 20 births annually per thousand of population (or 2.1 births per woman) are needed just to keep the population steady, in the absence of immigration.

- Figure 1 shows how Australia's birth rate has fallen steadily, despite some interesting peaks and troughs, over the last 130 years. Our reproduction rate fell below replacement in 1976 and has continued to decline since then. It is now 12 per cent below the long-term replacement rate (ABS, 1989b).

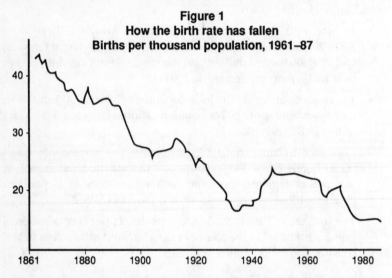

Figure 1
How the birth rate has fallen
Births per thousand population, 1961–87

Source: ABS, Australian Demographic Trends, Cat.3108.0, 1986, p.55

- Mothers of first children are older. Between 1956/60 and 1988, the median age of first-child mothers increased from 23.6 years to 27.1 years (ABS, 1989b).

Ex-Nuptial Births

- The ratio of ex-nuptial births to nuptial births has increased significantly. In 1971 they represented 9.3 per cent of total births, and by 1990 they represented just on 22 per cent of all births, comprising 57407 births out of an overall total of 262 648. Teenage ex-nuptial confinements constitute about 5 per cent of all confinements.

Chapter 3

Justice in Marriage and Divorce

Throughout the Western world, especially in the English-speaking portion of it, marriage is occurring later and breaking down more frequently. Many hypotheses have been advanced about causes but none has been proved. Several changes that are probably relevant have occurred more or less together, and it is difficult to say which might be causes and which effects.

Family law, and divorce law in particular, has changed; feminism as a social movement has had great social and political influence; female workforce participation and financial independence have grown rapidly; the reach of the welfare state and its provision of alternative sources of livelihood have advanced enormously, and along with this have come higher levels of unemployment and generally higher levels of taxation. Average family real and disposable income, especially for single-income families with dependent children, has remained static or fallen. The moral and cultural climate of 'traditional' family life has changed and the public treatment of sexual and erotic matters is noticeably different from that of a generation ago. The outcome is a drift towards changing family structures, revealed pre-eminently in changing attitudes towards marriage and its legal status.

The Marriage Relationship, Custom and Law

Marriage, so dictionaries tell us, is the legal union of a man and woman for life. The Family Law Act 1975 speaks of 'the need to preserve and protect the institution of marriage as the union of a man and a woman to the exclusion of all others voluntarily entered into for life' (section 43 (a)).

The state, as law-maker and enforcer, is involved in assessing the legal implications of the nature of marriage and in determining the conditions of its dissolution. As the guardian and enforcer of just relations in general between citizens, the state is likewise committed to overseeing just relations between the partners in marriage. We shall here be interested in exploring what constitutes just relations between husband and wife and the proper role of the state in guarding justice in that relationship. But we first need to understand what **kind** of relationship and institution marriage is.

13

Although law now governs marriage, law did not create it. The laws of marriage are more truly seen as an evolving response to, and codification of, folk practices, customs and expectations lodged deeply in the social history of northern Europe (Mount:1982). For at least 500 years, one of the characteristics of English marriage, in particular, has been its private, voluntary character and the freedom of choice of a marriage partner exercised by men and women. Although parents then (as now) might seek to mould the choices of their children, independence prevailed. Speaking of 15th-century England, Mount remarks (1982:75): 'Every parent's carefully laid plan for advancing the family's fortune was at the mercy of two young people simply deciding to **marry themselves** by the exchange of vows. All England was a vast Gretna Green, with the Church courts desperately trying to regulate, register and make indissoluble these "private marriages"'. The Church finally gained some of the controls it sought — which were eventually subsumed by the state — but not the power of determining choice. Much of its regulation reflected sentiments about marriage, and what was entailed in the 'vows' that were exchanged, that had a popular history of their own.

A distant echo of that history is to be found in Australia. In the early years of outback settlement, the isolation of homesteads and small communities, the difficulties of transport and the shortage of priests meant that many Catholic couples simply married themselves in the absence of priests and religious services. When the priest came, perhaps several years later, they would solemnise the marriage and baptise their children on the same day.

Formal law has less to say about the beginning of marriage than about its ending. This is not surprising. History shows that for the great mass of mankind no laws are needed to bring men and women together, to ensure procreation, to make parents love and care for their children, to decree love or mutual support and cooperation between men and women, or to initiate vows of mutual commitment. These aspirations spring unbidden from our humanity; and a framework, an 'institution', for their consummation is the prospect that 'marriage' holds out. But the nature of the aspirations is such that an adequate framework for their effective realisation must be an enduring one, or at least promise to be so; otherwise it is of little worth. And so the reference in the Family Law Act to marriage as a union 'voluntarily entered into for life' is no mere rhetorical flourish. The Act is pointing to institutional substance: to the presumption of permanence in marriage that distinguishes marriage from other forms of male-female relationships and commitments. The presumption, in the law, of the permanence of marriage and the corresponding intention of the marrying parties that it should be so, is the foundation upon which the 'binding union' and the distinctive legal character of marriage and its consequences have been built, even though that understanding has been significantly changed by recent modifications of family law.

The importance of the **intention** by the parties that the marriage should be permanent is crucial to the significance of the vows exchanged in marriage. Without it, promises of mutual care and fidelity are written in water and no way of life could confidently be built upon them. This is not to deny, however, that unpleasant and unforeseen realities may overtake the best intentions and the most honestly made vows. People change, people make mistakes about other people, changing circumstances have their effects, and sometimes things slowly unravel for all sorts of reasons and nobody is necessarily to blame; and so the reality of married life may often disappoint the hopes of those who enter it. That is life. Nevertheless, it is upon the legitimate expectations expressed in the vows and pledges that married life is erected. If they are meaningless, then marriage itself, as a distinct institution, is meaningless; if they are wilfully betrayed, a life built around belief in them is betrayed.

Marriage and Contract

Marriage, in this pledging sense, is a contract; a special kind of contract with elements unlike any other, as we shall see, but a contract nevertheless.

In law, a valid contract must have these features: voluntary offer and acceptance of the terms of the contract by the parties to it; a 'consideration', i.e. something of value exchanged by the parties; and intention to contract. Traditional marriage, insofar as the 'offer and acceptance' are voluntary, meets these criteria. The consideration is the offer to exchange mutual services ('love', 'honour', 'fidelity', 'care', etc.); and the 'intention' is made plain in the voluntary exchange of vows, including the intention that the arrangement will be a life-long one.

More generally, any contract is a promise by at least two parties to commit resources they own or control to some joint endeavour or transaction. They do so in the belief that some exchange or sharing of their resources or capacities, what each has to offer the other (the 'consideration'), will enable them both to achieve their individual ends more effectively and/or efficiently.

Well-formed and legally enforceable contractual arrangements increase the effectiveness of human action by extending the scope of cooperation and coordination, by enlarging the resources that can be mobilised to achieve shared goals, by increasing the predictability and certainty of contingent human action, and by lowering the risks of costly failures. This is readily apparent in the field of commerce. In addition to firm property rights, the growth of commerce has depended upon developing ways to lessen the risks of dishonesty and the failures of people to abide by their promises. Insurance policies, contracts and a legal apparatus to enforce them, and compensation for default and negligence are just a few of the devices that have encouraged the growth of commerce and enterprise by making transactions more efficient, and by reducing the risks and costs of human duplicity and failures of performance. As Rosenberg and Birdzell (1986:116) put it, 'there remains a striking contrast between a system of law which seeks to make the legal consequences of human action coherent and predictable and the many systems which either have no such objective or allow it to become lost among competing objectives'.

Good law helps make the 'legal consequences of human action coherent and predictable'; and it is important to note that one of the things that such law does is to impose systems of constraints. In ruling out certain kinds of action it makes possible other kinds of action of an enterprising and productive kind that might otherwise be inhibited by radical unpredictability of consequences, high risk, and the possibilities of damage to various persons' interests. Well-formed constraints, in short, can open up opportunities and be a condition of liberation and creativity.

When well-formed constraints (good laws) protect men and women from arbitrariness, exploitation and uncompensated deception or injury, they will be more prepared to make the investments of capital, energy, enthusiasm, creativity and devotion upon which the greatest of human enterprises depend. Conversely, when the law offers no such guarantees, we should not be surprised if there is no enterprise, or that it fails, achieves less than it is capable of, or delivers injustice to one party or another.

The 'Institution' of Marriage

The folk law or customary law that came to surround traditional marriage vows, and which came to form the substance of formal marriage law, provided protection and guarantees of the required kind. It summarised the rules governing a widespread and regular practice that we now understand as the 'institution' of marriage.

John Rawls (1971:55) has defined an institution thus:

Now by an institution I shall understand a public system of rules which defines offices and positions with their rights and duties, powers and immunities, and the like. These rules specify certain forms of action as permissible, others as forbidden; and they provide for certain penalties and defenses, and so on, when violations occur . . . An institution exists at a certain time and place when the actions specified by it are regularly carried out in accordance with a public understanding that the system of rules defining the institution is to be followed.

Marriage versus Cohabitation

Rawls's definition fits marriage — or did until recent changes. But, accepting it, we may understand 'traditional' marriage as contractual and institutional. Rawls goes on to say (1971:56):

The publicity of the rules of an institution insures that those engaged in it know what limitations on conduct to expect of one another and what kinds of actions are permissible. There is a common basis for determining mutual expectations.

The institution of marriage recognises, and the law confirms and formalises, the rules, the sanctions, the roles and the public understandings that have encrusted about a regular practice of a contractually distinctive kind — the marriage relationship. Among the 'mutual expectations' that define the contract and the institution, and which impose 'limitations on conduct', is (as noted above) the presumption by the parties, and their mutually declared intention, that the relationship will be permanent. It is this that crucially distinguishes marriage from cohabitation. It is the refusal or neglect to make a public and binding declaration of intention to establish a permanent relationship and contract that marks cohabitation. Although sexual union, companionship, a joint household, and even children, may be common to both marriage and cohabitation, cohabitation is the choice of a relationship that actively seeks to avoid the public promise of permanent bonding that is characteristic of marriage. In view of the greater frequency of divorce among those who have lived together before marriage, cohabiting couples may be more resistant to commitments of a permanent nature and thus more averse to sustaining a marriage. Such an aversion may underlie a need to seek the conflict that justifies ending the commitment.

Traditionally, 'de facto' or common-law marriage is a status that the law recognises as emerging from a cohabiting relationship that has taken on, by practices and relationships sustained over a reasonably long period, those characteristics, including spousal 'investments' and a presumption of intention to make the relationship permanent, that are (with the exception of the completion of the legal formalities) distinctive of marriage. So it becomes reasonable to infer that marriage has, in fact ('de facto'), taken place and, that being so, the law has an obligation to take account of that changed status and to include the parties within the requirements and protections that the law lays down for the formally married. Yet it must be said that this view of the differences between marriage and cohabitation would have been a more accurate description of the situation before the Family Law Act 1975 and some recent enactments by the States, principally New South Wales. Although the Family Law Act pays lip service to the conception of marriage as an exclusive union 'voluntarily entered into for life', this is not reflected in its substance, which draws no conclusions from this presumption of permanence and the investments made on that presumption by the marriage partners. Accordingly, the Family Law Act has significantly weakened, almost to the point of obliteration, the distinction between marriage and cohabitation, and some State laws have established rights and obligations between cohabiting partners, for example in respect of maintenance and custody of children, that follow those of marriage. The federal Act applies to children in all States, irrespective of whether the parents are married or de facto married partners. So the present situation is ambiguous, confusing and non-uniform. In this, it reflects the prevailing uncertainty about the institutional status of marriage and whether, and if so how, it differs from cohabitation or concubinage.

Functions and Consequences of Marriage

But the public perception of difference remains, and we must ask why so many men and women continue to seek marriage in the traditional sense rather than cohabitation. What does this form of male-female relationship offer that cohabitation does not?

To such a question there is both a plain answer and a deeper one. The plain answer, which is in part a common-sense response to the presumption of a permanent and onerous commitment, is that the act of marriage is seen as offering guarantees of continuity and mutual good faith matching the importance of the 'investments' put at stake in a marriage. Somewhat like the legal forms available to commercial transactions under well-formed law, it is believed to reduce the risks of losing the benefits expected to flow from substantial investments. The benefits foreseen in marriage and the presumption of its permanence include continuity of exclusive sexual enjoyment, constant companionship, mutual care, a jointly supported household, the advantages of some division of labour, children, cooperative and stable rearing of children, and joint endeavours to advance their interests. None of this is possible without emotional commitments and joint investments of time, effort and money. One partner's investments can be rendered nugatory by failures of performance, or the active hostility, of the other partner. Such risks may be reduced, if not eliminated, by marriage vows carrying enforceable penalties or compensations for non-performance.

The deeper answer to the question 'why marriage?' cannot be given so plainly and practically. It takes us beyond those basic expectations that can be roughly (but importantly) encompassed in a form of contract to the human urge to immerse oneself in an open-ended and continuing relationship of mutual care and intimate involvement with unforeseeable but yearned-for ramifications.

But to return to the theme we wish to pursue: marriage, when it is genuinely contractual with terms that may be enforced or be subject to compensation for non-performance, differs markedly from non-contractual cohabitation. Marriage involves a bond with a presumption of permanency and its meaning is inseparable from its 'bonding' nature. If the bonds and constraints that sustain and uphold marriage are eliminated, so is marriage as a public institution, no matter what other formalities and rituals might be retained.

Marriage in this bonding sense offers an **alternative** way of life to cohabitation. Both are voluntary, and each has its attractions for different people under different circumstances. But if the distinction between them is eliminated, an alternative has been lost and the possibilities of life are accordingly impoverished. As suggested above, well-formed constraints may be liberating: they may construct the framework for otherwise impossible forms of enterprise, enrichment and fulfilment; they create the more secure and predictable environment in which real and durable **choices** may take place. When we lose the constraints we lose choice; we lose a species of liberty and the guarantees that underwrite the unique and productive environment that marriage can create.

Bonding and Unbonding

The voluntariness and privacy of the decision by a couple to get married, to accept marital bonding, are crucial to the character of the bonding itself. Their decision to 'marry' is then given social or institutional affirmation and recognition in a publicly witnessed exchange of vows in the ceremony and 'registration' of marriage and in the consequently altered legal identity of the parties. But the bond itself is **theirs**, jointly. They are the only ones who can **unite** themselves. But if the bond itself is their joint creation, and theirs alone, it follows that they may, jointly, unbond themselves if that, too, should be their common wish; provided they freely and jointly consent to the terms of the unbonding and provided there are no third-party effects of the unbonding (such as the consequences for their children) that should, in justice, be taken into account. If these conditions are met, the possibility of divorce by mutual consent presents no problems of principle. Indeed, in preserving the private and voluntary character of the bonding relationship, divorce is really an affirmation of that aspect of marriage rather than a denial or subversion of it. It preserves the **choice** that marriage offers. Naturally, the formalities needed to bring about an altered legal status must again be completed and registered, but it needs no more than this.

If all of this is true, it follows, however, that unilateral unbonding is not permissible or justifiable. One-party repudiation cannot be a **joint** unbonding, only the breaking of a contract. Where mutual consent is absent, the non-repudiating party may properly raise an issue of justice that the state cannot, or should not, ignore: namely, that legitimate expectations formed under the contract have been betrayed, causing damage.

Where one party wishes to exit the marriage and the other party claims broken contract, two separate issues are raised, which should not be confused. There should be no legal impediment preventing a party from freely ending a marriage, but there is every reason why a claim by the other party that promises have been broken, and damage incurred, should be heard. In short, divorce should be readily available but broken promises should be paid for at the same time; fault is not an issue in divorce but it is an issue affecting the terms of the divorce settlement, of the winding-up of the marriage contract.

Ancient Rights in Marriage and Divorce

With varying degrees of formality and elaboration, this view of marriage and divorce has very ancient credentials. In his discussion of divorce, Mount points to the relative freedom and informality of entry into and exit from marriage in Roman, pre-Christian and early Christian Europe. But he also describes the protection given by enforcement of custom and law to the interests and legitimate expectations of the affected parties. In ancient Babylon, for instance, 'a man might always divorce his wife at will, but he had to restore her dowry and provide for the maintenance of the children' (Mount, 1982:202). A few lines later, Mount records: 'Pre-Christian societies in general recognize two rights: the underlying right of individuals to divorce and remarry, and the right of compensation and maintenance of those adversely affected by the divorce'.

No less a Christian and Puritan conscience than John Milton's acknowledged (Mount, 1982:210) that: 'Love in marriage cannot love nor subsist unless it be mutual; and where love cannot be, there can be left of wedlock nothing but the empty husk of an outside matrimony, as undelightful and unpleasing to God as any other kind of hypocrisy'. And further on (Mount, 1982:211):

> For although differences in divorce about dowries, jointures, and the like, besides the punishing of adultery, ought not to pass without referring, if need be, to the magistrate; yet that the absolute and final hindering of divorce cannot belong to any civil or earthly power, against the will of both parties, or of the husband alone.

Although we would now include the will of 'the wife alone', this is a conception of marriage and divorce by the author of *Four Treatises on Divorce* that does justice to the liberties of the parties, to their obligations to each other, and to the integrity, as well as the vicissitudes, of the central human bond between men and women that affirms them both and cradles their happiness.

Justice in Divorce

The right to divorce is as precious as the right to get married. All rights imply obligations, and the obligations of marriage should be matched, indeed mirrored, by the obligations that attend divorce, which is the right to undo justly the obligations of marriage.

If marriage as we have defined it has an indispensable role to play in human fulfilment and social well-being, that role depends absolutely upon the availability of justice in divorce. There is an indissoluble link between confidence and success in marriage, and confidence that, if it should fail, all will not be lost because of injustice. For, if marriage is

21

a meaningful commitment, then something **valuable** must be committed; important investments are put at risk. The success of any marriage depends on these investments, which are less likely to be made and the marriage less likely to be successful if the risk of the investments being irretrievably lost is high. As well, if both parties know that wilful or careless dereliction of what is due to the other will surely entail at least some remedying of the damage done, and the continuation of some of the obligations (e.g. child maintenance), then damage is less likely to be done and the obligations less likely to be abandoned. The law cannot help being a moral educator of one kind or another. If it says that the responsibilities of marriage may be unilaterally abandoned, that is the morality it teaches and confirms. If it says rights will be protected and obligations enforced, it teaches the morality of respect for rights and obligations and demands that respect. Most people understand and acknowledge this and, as the quotations above show, it is ancient wisdom long enshrined in custom and law.

If we wish to be even-handed about both the obligations of marriage and the right to divorce, 'fault' in not meeting the obligations of the marriage contract should be cause for legal concern, for referring to Milton's 'magistrate', only if one party raises it as a cause of damage to that party in divorce proceedings initiated by either party. It must be emphasised, therefore, that the issue is not whether a divorce decree will be made, but only whether damages will be awarded, upon divorce, against a party who has deliberately betrayed the legitimate expectations of the other party based upon the bond and contract enacted in entering the married state.

'Betrayal', to be actionable, must involve wilful disappointment of the reasonable benefits normally expected of the married state. Failure of sexual consummation, for instance, has long been recognised as justifying annulment or divorce (although no longer relevant as a ground in Australia), but would not necessarily be actionable for damages if it could be shown to be involuntary. But adultery, being necessarily a wilful betrayal of the legitimate expectation of sexual fidelity, would be actionable. Similarly with cruelty or desertion, or other voluntary failures of performance that destroy the essential foundations of the bond.

The view presented here of the nature of marriage, and of the rights and obligations at stake in marriage and divorce, hinges on the fundamental proposition that marriage is truly an 'exchange of vows' establishing contractual rights and legitimate expectations between the parties. In most successful marriages it comprises much more that cannot be caught in ordinary notions of contract; but it is **at least** that. If it were not, it would be little more than a form of cohabitation.

We are only now beginning to realise that recent changes in the law give inadequate recognition to the truth about marriage and divorce and how these changes have robbed us of the liberating constraints and the legal supports of the alternative way of life that genuine marriage creates. Above all, we are now witnessing the Pandora's box of injustice and judicial arbitrariness that has been opened up.

Chapter 4

Marriage and Divorce in Modern Law

Before 1959, marriage and divorce law was the province of the Australian States, although the Commonwealth had the constitutional power, hitherto unexercised, to legislate in this area. The federal Matrimonial Causes Act 1959 was the first exercise of the federal powers, followed shortly after by the Marriage Act 1961. It listed 14 grounds upon which a divorce might be sought. In the main, these grounds comprised voluntary acts — adultery, cruelty, habitual drunkenness, etc. — or voluntary derelictions, such as desertion, that were taken to constitute 'faults' so serious as to justify the offended party suing for divorce, on the grounds that his or her marital rights and expectations under the marriage had been betrayed. The radically revised Family Law Act 1975 created a single ground for divorce — irretrievable breakdown of the marriage demonstrated by one year's separation — and jettisoned all notions of fault or betrayal; these were not mentioned and became wholly irrelevant to the divorce petition and to the divorce settlement.

This new Act, promoted by an Attorney-General and a federal government dedicated to reform, was a child of its times. Before the Act was passed, there was widespread dissatisfaction with the hypocrisy and deceit required to win a divorce by couples who were in agreement that their marriage had failed. For those parties innocent of fault who simply wanted a parting of the ways, there was no alternative but to manufacture the evidence of 'fault' by colluding in contrived bedroom 'discoveries' of adultery, for example. Many people were disgusted by the parade of marital and extra-marital conflicts and intimacies in the divorce courts which were duly, and often salaciously, reported in the press. 'No fault' divorce had already become law in California in 1970. The time was ripe for wiping away the vestiges of four centuries of church and state control over the right to divorce.

Objectives of the Family Law Act

These movements towards change coalesced in a number of objectives animating the reformers: to remove the legal barriers and costs preventing dignified and consensual divorces and, in so doing, to restore divorce as a realistically available right; to absolve the courts from enquiring into the causes of marital breakdown; to 'liberalise' divorce by expunging notions of 'fault' and 'guilt'; and to simply allow the institution of marriage to endure voluntarily through 'strong' marriages because divorce was irrelevant to them anyway. Easier, 'no fault' divorce was intended to be a humane way of quickly and decently burying dead marriages without interfering with those that were alive and well. The idea that marriage was simply a ritual act of 'commitment' evincing love (at least for the time being), and no more than that, became widespread. The old, common-sense understanding that marriage was a complex mixture of sentiment, pragmatism, mutual trust, trade-offs, generativity and economics, dependent upon a subtle balancing of costs and benefits, of positive and negative incentives, fell victim to an odd combination of genuine liberalism, romanticism and ideology.

In so seeking to make divorce simpler and less painful (admirable objectives, other things being equal), the Act destroyed the **contractual** character of marriage by allowing dissolution of the marriage bond without the possibility of examining whether a party may have suffered damage by breaking of the marriage contract. It is one thing to eliminate 'fault' as a **ground** for divorce, but quite another thing explicitly to forbid its being raised as a relevant issue in a divorce **settlement**. Trainor (1992) has similarly emphasised the contractual character of marriage and the Act's betrayal of that character, and hence justice, in an important article that further argues for the restoration of what he describes as the 'democratic compromise' between liberal and conservative concerns in marriage and divorce law.

Divorce and the Meaning of Marriage

In ordinary circumstances, the great majority of men and women, when they marry, willingly undertake commitments that they would not contemplate outside the married state. American research has shown, for example, that single, separated and divorced men of all races work 20 per cent fewer hours than married men (Gilder, 1981:133).

The daily, practical reality of most marriages is hard work for both men and women. It involves dozens of forms of household cooperation, division of labour and mutual care. Women will have children in marriage when the majority would not consider it outside marriage because they believe marriage creates a secure and supportive haven for child-bearing and raising. Husbands and fathers will work long hours, and build and maintain houses with an enthusiasm and sense of involvement that they would not have if they were single. A Wisconsin study has shown that the work of married men increases with age, education, job experience and birth of children, and that husbands work 50 per cent harder than bachelors of comparable age, education and skills (Gilder, 1981:69).

For wives or husbands who take the major responsibility for home and child care, and even more so if they are full or part-time members of the industrial workforce, the burden of work is immense. This, for the great majority, is what marriage is all about; it is what is expected; it is part of the 'deal' that has been voluntarily made. And the making and meeting of commitments in these ways is the substance of the reciprocal and complementary investments made in marriage by men and women.

However, when one partner faithfully sticks to the deal and the other partner defaults by breaking the vows or simply by walking away from the marriage without good cause, all that has been done by one partner in service to the union, all that has been built and committed in good faith, may be unilaterally nullified by the other partner. What we would never for a moment condone in a commercial relationship is routinely ignored in one of the most important of all human relationships. The compact at its heart has been betrayed and an injustice done for which the Family Law Act has no remedy or compensation — not only by side-stepping its obligation to judge the contractual performances of the marriage partners, but also, as we shall see, by ignoring the rule of law as we are accustomed to understanding it.

Marriage needs just law, but marriage law has cast justice aside.

The Marriage Contract and Modern Law

In acknowledging the contractual element of marriage we must beware of going too far. It is quite unreal and potentially dangerous to attempt to **reduce** marriage and family relationships entirely to contractual terms. Such relationships bring with them unstatable and unforeseeable obligations whose imperatives, no matter how 'unfair' and burdensome they might sometimes be, simply cannot be dismissed as contractually unconscionable. To take a wife or a husband, or to have a child is, in all sorts of respects, a leap in the dark with unimaginable and non-negotiable consequences that make the idea of contracting into or out of them laughable. Where is the contract that can sensibly say **how much** care a husband should give to a sick wife, or wife to husband? At what point — destitution? exhaustion? sacrificing his or her own life? — does a parent 'reasonably' desist from attempts to save the life of a sick or threatened son or daughter? When are the terms of the contract 'exceeded'? No contract is capable of describing or containing the meanings of kinship and the actual life of families.

Parenting, in particular, carries biologically based status obligations that cannot properly be alienated by contract — such as 'lending' a womb to contract the gestation of 'somebody else's' child. What is in the womb is the child of the owner of that womb.

But apart from all else, marriage is a social creation and tradition, not an artefact fashioned merely by promises and agreements generated by consenting individuals. In an obvious sense, marriage is a voluntary association with contractual elements. But that is a thin description of an institution that presents its 'terms' ready-made, though ultimately indeterminate, to men and women who are ready to be captured by it. Marriage, in this sense, is already there and waiting to give form and articulation to commitments and a way of life beyond the capacities of individual men and women fully to imagine, let alone formulate and agree upon, for themselves.

These considerations are what Hegel had in mind when he spoke of marriage as 'a contract to transcend the standpoint of contract' (Knox, 1945:112). Marriage is at least a contract, but there is more to it than can ever be captured in contractual terms, and to pretend to do so would be dangerously to diminish it. The contractual base and vows of marriage can do no more (important though it is) than set the framework or, if you like, the 'grammatical rules' in conformity with which the infinitely varied 'utterances' of daily married life may be made. But the futility of attempting to draft a realistic and fully definitive marriage contract does not mean that something less ambitious might not be possible and valuable.

Private Marriage or Public Rules?

In contemplating the recent major changes in marriage law in the English-speaking countries, some have raised the question whether the regulatory retreat from marriage by the state presages an era of private marriage contracts (Horton & Alexander, 1986:229–55). Norman Barry, for example, has suggested the 'privatisation' of marriage by repealing most of the marriage laws:

> Marriage should be governed by the common law of contract and divorce treated as a type of breach of contract. The form of marriage contract that people can make should be limited only by statutory provisions to protect children and laws to outlaw such things as bigamous marriage contracts. Just how property should be distributed, questions of the care and custody of children and future maintenance payments would be settled by prior agreement. (Barry, 1988:39)

Barry's proposals arise out of his consideration of the increasing frequency of divorce and the reasons for it, among which he notes the recent weakening of the contractual-type constraints present in the former marriage and divorce laws and the increasing independence of women, which have created stronger incentives for divorce. He thus recognises the significance of the contractual element and the consequences of its weakening. But it is also worth noting that he sees an essential role for some statutory scaffolding to affirm the **special** character of marriage contracts. Barry is moving in the same direction as I wish to go, except that I see a more important role for basic statutory provisions in **defining** the institution of marriage than he would seem to allow.

For example, if Barry's proposals were carried out, would we be likely to see a strong movement towards contracts more exacting than the marriage contract under the present law? Would individuals seek to reintroduce enforceable sanctions for adultery, cruelty, desertion, etc.? Would they pay particular attention to defining rights to property, access, and custody of children? The whole history of the marriage relationship suggests that this is highly likely, for the simple reason, as we have argued, that these things go to the heart of the sort of relationship that men and women seek through **marriage**. Moreover, the recent growth in Australia of contracts to govern de facto marriage relationships (Barry, 1988:39) and the more frequent drafting of pre-marriage property agreements are evidence of the things people see as important in such relationships and the circumstances of their dissolution.

In other words, people have a 'core' idea of marriage and its obligations in their heads that marks it as a distinct area for a particular kind of contract. If the law is to support that common understanding it needs to reconstitute what Rawls describes as that 'public system of rules' characteristic of genuine institutions. I would argue, therefore, that there are two main possibilities: either to allow individual men and women to forge their own marriage contracts along the lines suggested by Barry, or to alter family law so that broken marriage vows may become an issue in the divorce settlement and be made grounds for damages suits and forms of compensation. For the reasons sketched above, I would favour the latter course of expressing in statute law the common core idea of marriage and its obligations, especially to children, with which the majority would rest content. This would be simpler and more modestly realistic, while still allowing a third possibility — to permit supplementary contracts to be made between the partners, provided they are consistent with these basic provisions.

Under existing law, no pre-nuptial contract can stand if it is inconsistent with the present provisions of the Family Law Act.

The Effects of Legal Changes on the Divorce Rate

The fact that the divorce rate has more than doubled since the passage of the Family Law Act 1975 suggests at least two possibilities that are not necessarily incompatible: first, that the Act, in removing the former difficulties of divorce, has allowed unhappy couples to part more easily; and second, that the Act itself has created uncertainties and incentives that undermine the marriage bond. A third possibility is that changes in the law have not been the major factor and that the steadily increasing rate of divorce (which began **before** the new Act) may be due to underlying social and economic trends operating independently of the law but being reflected in it. Alan Tapper explores this possibility acutely and in some detail. After examining a number of possible contributing factors and hypotheses about causes, he concludes that

> we may be left with a threefold phenomenon: traditional male emotional immaturity; the stresses of women's growing public independence, combined with a possible loss of understanding about private life; and the intervention of the welfare system, in a way which was (and is) biased against two-parent families. These may be enough to explain the two other important questions that arise here: Why is it that women instigate separations; and why these tend to happen so early in marriage. (Tapper, 1990a:174)

I will not pursue in detail the causes of the rise in divorce rates, but it is relevant to my purpose to place divorce in the context of the law and the pressures arising from economic change and the burden of the welfare state on the independence of families. These latter issues will be taken up again after I have concluded the discussion of marital law. Meanwhile, it is worth noting the statistical relationship between rising divorce and falling fertility, a relationship that occurs also in some other Western societies, such as Britain, the United States and Sweden. In Australia, while the fertility rate fell from an average of 3.41 children per woman in 1956–60 to 1.84 in 1988 (ABS, 1989b), the divorce rate climbed from 0.7 divorces per 1000 marriages in 1956–60 to 2.5 in 1988. Associated with this is the fact that the percentage of divorces that involve children has fallen from 68 per cent in 1974 to 57.5 per cent in 1988 (ABS,1989d). Put another way, families without children are more likely to divorce, and the increase in divorce over that period is concentrated in childless families. Since childless couples tend to be young couples, this would at least partly explain why separations are more common in the early stages of marriage. No conclusions about causality can be inferred from the figures quoted above, but they do suggest that there may be a more fundamental factor or group of factors contributing to both falling fertility and rising divorce. It is not surprising that the presence of children, especially young children, is more likely to keep couples together. But it is interesting to speculate whether a major socio-economic trend, such as declining relative disposable incomes of married couples, is the more fundamental contributing factor.

Whether or not this is so, it is at least plausible to suggest that the impact or 'valency' of whatever these underlying social and/or economic factors might be is intensified by the removal of the contractual constraints formerly operating within marriage. Other things remaining equal, easier divorce would tend to raise the divorce rate. This is supported by the fact that, although the divorce rate was rising before the Family Law Act 1975, and given due allowance for the 'backlog' effect suddenly raising the divorce statistics for 1976–78, the rate of divorce settled down in the late 1970s and 1980s at a significantly higher level (2.5 times higher) than the pre-1976 rate. It can scarcely be seriously argued that the removal of important behavioural constraints by the new Act has had no behavioural consequences, but how large they are and how they operate is something that needs to be investigated. It is to such questions that we now turn.

Ending a Marriage

Under present circumstances, if a husband and wife without children are both eager to divorce, and agree on questions of property and maintenance, and so on, they simply have to separate for a year and then petition for a divorce, which will normally be granted without undue delay or difficulty. Such free, consensual arrangements, I have argued, protect the privacy and voluntariness of their relationship and, in these circumstances, the present law deals fairly with the parties.

If one party wishes to divorce and the other does not, there is nothing the reluctant party can do to prevent a divorce. I have also argued that such a divorce should nevertheless continue to proceed, provided that neither party wishes to accuse the other of dereliction, in one respect or another, of the marriage 'vows' as traditionally understood. However, if one party does wish to make such an accusation, this raises an issue of crucial importance that cannot be swept aside. Where I believe it should lead will be discussed later on.

If parties agree to divorce, but cannot agree on the disposition of property, or maintenance, or questions of custody and access, the court becomes involved. Anecdotes in the press (e.g. *The Sydney Morning Herald*, 1991b) and the many volumes of submissions to the Federal Parliamentary Joint Select Committee on Certain Aspects of the Operation and Interpretation of the Family Law Act, 1991–92, provide evidence of the often expensive and extended litigation, and bitterness between the parties, that frequently arise in these cases. Such adversarial conflicts occur in only a minority of divorces, but they nevertheless amount to several thousand cases annually. This is a substantial number and presumably includes litigants who are unreasonable and unwilling to compromise, thus forcing their partners to litigation, as well as those who are simply seeking justice from the court. It is the vicissitudes of this group in particular that have directed attention to the Family Court and its interpretation and administration of the Act.

The Family Court and its Powers

In addition to the bombing and murder that have been aimed at the Court and its judges, widespread criticism of difficulties and injustices in the proceedings of the court have been expressed by litigants and observers (see, for example, the submissions to the Joint Parliamentary Select Committee referred to above) and, more dispassionately, by lawyers themselves (Fagan, 1990). Central to these problems are the indeterminacy and uncertainty of many aspects of family law arising from the extreme discretion that the Act confers on Family Court judges.

In an important article on these matters, Sydney barrister Desmond Fagan (1990:12) points out that the Family Law Act 'leaves the resolution of virtually every dispute within its scope to the discretion of a single judge', and he adds that it is 'fundamentally against the public interest that this body of law should consist entirely of discretions conferred upon single judges'. Fagan's points may be paraphrased thus:

• Under such a discretionary system, the outcome of matrimonial litigation is quite unpredictable; such discretion and the dearth of clear rules make the law in this area highly uncertain; lawyers cannot confidently advise their clients of their rights and the probability of success or otherwise in a case; unreasonable litigants are encouraged by this uncertainty not to settle, and costs become exorbitant.

- Settlement of disputes without litigation is more likely to occur when the law is certain and predictable.

- Discretionary judgments are likely to be seen as **personal** decisions by judges rather than the impersonal application of rules of law to facts established.

- Since there is no way of knowing in advance which marital facts might be considered relevant by a judge, a large range of factual issues can be canvassed, making the whole case fluid and drawn out.

These are fundamental criticisms of the substance (or lack of it) of family law and its effects upon those unfortunate enough to come before the court over their matrimonial matters. It corroborates our earlier remark that the Family Law Act, in so elevating judicial discretion, has little in common with the rule of law as we have come to know it. In 1970, upholding an appeal to the House of Lords against a **discretionary** judgment by Lord Denning under the English Married Woman's Property Act 1882, Lord Hodson said that to dismiss the appeal, 'would be to substitute the uncertain and crooked cord of discretion for the golden and straight metwand [i.e. measuring rod] of the law' (Denning, 1980:209).

Family Law is not 'straight and golden'; its continuing problem is that it is silent on matters where it should speak, and is often evasive and ambiguous where it does. The Act is thus defective in two main respects. First, it leaves too much to judicial discretion. Second, it provides neither legal remedy nor compensation for those who suffer from broken marital contracts, and accordingly mocks its own characterisation of the nature of the marriage relationship as 'solemn and binding' (s.46(1)).

These deficiencies are discussed in Chapter 5.

Chapter 5

Restoring Certainty and
Justice to Family Law

T he first of the defects referred to above is open to remedy by
drafting specific rules to govern matters presently left to judicial
discretion. As Fagan points out (1990:14), 'there is no reason
why a set of rules could not be formulated based upon the experience
of the Family Court in the thousands of cases which have been
decided by it under the 1975 Act'. Under the Act, the main areas of
adversarial contention are property, maintenance, custody and access. In each of these areas there is no *a priori* reason why clear rules
could not be established to yield the benefits of certainty and
predictability referred to earlier.

Mothers, Fathers and Child Custody

In the matter of custody, for example, it would seem that the obvious
point of departure in thinking about it should be the recognition that
both parents have natural rights of 'ownership' of their child or
children and that these rights are in no way abrogated by a divorce
in which violence, abuse, desertion or neglect is not an issue.
However, the fact that only the mother has carriage of the embryonic
child for the first nine months and has a biologically-driven and
special role in the first few months after birth suggests a justifiable
claim to something more than exactly equal 'ownership'. There is
also the simple fact that mothers in general invest a great deal more
time in child care than fathers (ABS, 1987). Scientific evidence
suggests that this customary practice and the maternal 'bonding' that
normally goes with it are important for healthy child development
(Bowlby, 1982). It would seem contrary to justice and the public
interest to ignore all this simply to impose an ideological conception
of sexual equivalence that is not supported by the facts in this
particular matter. Such a view would seem to be in tune with the
common public opinion that mothers are normally more intensely
committed to close care of children than fathers.

The **formal** stance of the Family Court is apparently one of
neutrality over the claims of mothers and fathers in custody cases,
with neither being given *a priori* preference. According to
Finlay's authoritative analysis of the present state of family law

judgments (1989:232), the Court now takes 'the view that there is no longer any presumption favouring one parent or the other'. This represents a departure from traditional judicial views, such as those of Sir John Romilly in 1865, quoted by Finlay (1989:233) that 'Nothing and no person, and no combination of them, can in my opinion, with regard to a child of tender years, supply the place of a mother'. Or, more recently, the observation by the High Court of Australia in 1961, quoted by Finlay (1989:233):

> What is left is the strong presumption which is not of law but is founded on experience and upon the nature of ordinary human relationships, that a young child, particularly a girl, should have the love, care and attention of the child's mother and that her upbringing should be the responsibility of her mother, if it is not possible to have the responsibility of both parents living together.

However, despite its formal neutrality, the Family Court's practice is to favour the mother. In this it follows international practice, as indicated in Table 1.

Table 1

Comparison of results in several custody outcome studies in other countries and Australia (Family Court of Australia)

Studies	Custody/care and control of all children granted to:					
	Consent cases			Defended cases		
Mother, father, other	Moth	Fath	Oth	Moth	Fath	Oth
Doyle & Caron (1979) USA	84%	13%	3%	60%	35%	5%
Eekalaar & Clive (1979) UK	85%	8%	7%	53%	26%	21%
Maidment (1981) USA	87%	13%	0%	61%	39%	0%
Pearson, Munson & Thoennes (1982) UK	52%	17%	32%	39%	28%	33%
Weitzman & Dixon (1979) USA	90%	6%	4%	67%	33%	0%
Horwill & Bordow (1983) FCOA	79%	18%	3%	54%	31%	15%
Bordow (1992) FCOA	Not available			60%	31%	9%

Source: Joint Select Committee on Certain Aspects of the Operation & Interpretation of the Family Law Act. Submissions & Incorporated Documents, Vol. 29, S. 5731

The position is, then, that the law as it stands pretends to take a stance that is not supported by its practice, which is more or less to follow conventional and traditional wisdom in favouring the mother as custodian. In this it misleads; it is uncertain from the perspective of litigants and, indeed, encourages litigation by its uncertainty.

Public opinion would probably endorse a rule of law that always gave a mother custody of a child after divorce unless she were shown to be deserting, incompetent or abusive. In other words, the law would be explicitly saying that 'natural right' favours the mother as custodian after divorce. The adoption of such a rule, on these grounds, would absolve judges of the Family Court of the need to exercise a personal or paternalistic discretion hinging on their judgment of which parent would serve 'the best interests' of the child. Instead, the judge would be instructed, in effect, that society had already made that judgment in favour of mothers in general. None of this implies that fathers are incapable of giving children, even very young children, the deepest love and the tenderest of care. It is simply the judgment that, on the whole, mothers do it better, for reasons that are no doubt a subtle mixture of biology and culture, but which are powerful reasons nevertheless.

But, having said that, the rights of the father (and of children to **have** a father and the distinctive contribution that fathers make to their development) also need to be protected. The law in practice acknowledges the principle of joint guardianship (i.e. the continuation of the parental rights enjoyed during marriage) and normally permits a competent, non-abusive father to have access to his children, but no right to do so is recognised. Perhaps such a right should be explicitly recognised and precisely defined in terms of a minimum fraction of the year (perhaps one third) during which he should be able to be in the company of his children unless the children, at age 14, seek other arrangements.

This proposal of one third of the year (i.e. a **total** period of four months, not necessarily taken as a single period) as a statutory access entitlement for fathers not disqualified on grounds of incompetence or abuse would not, on the face of it, involve particular difficulties. It might, in fact, make many access arrangements easier. But some flexibility where needed should not pose an insuperable problem. Such a statutory entitlement would not, of course, prevent the parents from making whatever consensual custody and access agreements that suited them; the point is simply to declare the basic arrangements that will apply when the parents cannot agree among themselves. Nor would it prevent the making of a rule that qualified custody and access rights of parents, male or female, whose demonstrated character, habitual actions or relationships were likely to endanger the health, welfare or normal development of a child.

Property and Maintenance in Marriage and Divorce

Our purpose here is not to engage in a discussion of the details of marriage law, but to emphasise the importance of clear rules of law based upon consistent principles that can be defended, and also the importance of effective enforcement that is even-handed between men and women except where different treatment can be adequately justified. Along the same lines, therefore, one might argue for more certainty in questions of property and maintenance.

Fagan has suggested (1990:14), simply to illustrate this general point, that 'there might be a strict rule that the parties would be equally entitled to all property which had been acquired since the commencement of the marriage'. One can immediately think of factors that might complicate the actual determination of 'property acquired' after a certain date, especially if one or both parties had been bent on concealment for some time. But these are not, in principle, beyond the ingenuity of the law to anticipate and to counter, if necessary, with penalties.

The general principle of equal ownership of all assets acquired after marriage seems fair. But special caution should be exercised about the fate of the family home at divorce, particularly if children are involved, but even when they are not. The selling of the family home in order to divide assets equally can sometimes be a disaster for custodial parents and their children, or for wives for whom the home is the centre of life. Similar caution should be exercised in relation to businesses (including farms) that have been the main financial supports of spouses and children.

Property Owned Before Marriage

It might also turn out to be desirable to institute the option for marrying parties to declare, at marriage, which of their possessions they wished to exclude from this common pool. It might be said that to formalise this in marriage law would be to undermine the whole idea of marriage as a permanent union by immediately raising the spectre of its dissolution. But this is not necessarily so; it depends entirely upon the reasons why the parties might wish to raise the issue. If, on the one hand, the intention is clearly to protect the interests of third parties, such as children by a former marriage, parents or grandparents, business associates, or so on, then the other partner could judge the motives and their significance accordingly, and, on the other hand, no doubt judge differently if the motive is patently a self-serving and deliberately excluding one. Indeed, the exercise of such a prerogative by a prospective marriage partner would provide evidence about his or her character of value to the other party. Contrary to the suggestion that such a provision might be divisive, it would be an option that could work in the opposite direction and carry considerable moral force in concretising the 'union' and commitment of marriage by allowing the parties a **choice** that, no matter how it is made, reveals a great deal before the marriage is sealed; and that can only work in the direction of more realistic and better-informed marriages.

As suggested, such a provision could also be used to protect third-party interests (the bride's or groom's parents, for instance) in property or other assets implicated in the marriage, such as a family business, a loan, or a house. In combination with a strict rule about marital property acquired after marriage, it would greatly reduce the scope for property disputes at divorce. (Later on, I will add a qualification to the principle of equal division of property at the divorce settlement that should be made when one of the parties to the marriage has been shown to have broken the marriage contract.) There is, too, much to be said for the view that it is contrary to the essence of the marriage bargain to seek to discriminate between the 'value' of financial and property contributions to the marriage, on the one hand, as against the 'value' of household production and care of children, on the other. In most marriages, the earning capacity of the husband, for example, is inseparable from the work and care of the wife, and it ought to follow from this that the wife has a stake in his superannuation, or at least that portion of the entitlement acquired during the marriage. In practice, this would probably amount to the Court deciding on a monetary or property equivalent.

Be all of this as it may, the important task is to articulate fair, workable and defensible principles to serve as a secure (or as secure as possible) basis of certainty to ameliorate the pernicious consequences of the present uncertainty and judicial discretion. Doing so would also eliminate the conflict-engendering and contentious burden presently placed upon the court of assessing the relative 'contributions' of the parties to matrimonial assets, and the 'means and needs' of the parties.

Maintenance After Divorce

The question of spousal and child maintenance raises many complex problems that would be difficult to resolve even if clear principles were available to help the judicial decisions on these issues. But the present family law on the matter is bedevilled by confusion of principles and the resort to judicial assessment of what is 'fair in the circumstances' in isolation from any consideration of the responsibilities of parties for creating the circumstances in question. We would argue that the issue of maintenance cannot be justly separated from the marital rights and obligations of the parties and should therefore be considered as one part of a divorce settlement that may take questions of broken contract, of 'fault', into account. So we must turn now to this second of the main aspects of the deficiencies of the Family Law Act to which we referred at the end of Chapter 4 and to the unavoidable question of justice between the parties which it raises.

Broken Marriage Contracts and the Divorce Settlement

If marriage, even if only in a minimal sense, is a contractual relationship, it is absurd that the question of conduct within marriage contrary to the contract should be wholly irrelevant to the settlement attending its dissolution. Nothing could be more subversive of justice in the relationships between citizens in any of their dealings, let alone in marriage, than to propose that contract-breaking behaviour is of no interest to the law. And nothing could be more cruelly designed to provide an incentive for such behaviour than for the law to ignore it.

If, then, desertion of a marital partner, or cruelty or infidelity, for example, are breaches of contract in a marital context, the law should take note of it and allow it to play a part in determining the damage that has been done to a spouse who has suffered under this behaviour when a settlement is under consideration. It should therefore be open to a spouse to claim damages, at a divorce settlement, against a partner who has allegedly broken one or more of the basic undertakings between spouses that would be written into a revised Family Law Act. This is not the place to debate in detail what should constitute the breaking of 'basic undertakings', but let us assume that they would at least include adultery, cruelty, desertion, habitual intoxication, and abuse and/or neglect of children. The accusing spouse would, of course, be obliged to prove the accusation. If it is not proved, then the divorce would be settled upon ordinary terms decided within the framework of greater certainty and specificity in matters of property and custody that I have recommended above.

If the accusations are not contested, or if they are proved through adversarial encounter or judicial inquisition, there are two possibilities: the damaged partner may rest content with a finding of fault and may choose not to pursue the question of damages, which it would be open for him or her to do; or that party could pursue a claim for damages that the Court would then assess in a fashion consistent with the legal principles pertaining to civil damages for breach of contract. The main purpose would be to adequately compensate a spouse for what he or she has lost — the 'sunk costs', so to speak — by the dissolution of the marriage and by the disappointment of the ordinary expectations founded on the presumption of permanence of the marriage.

In practice, it is to be expected that damages will comprise property adjustments and money payments and entitlements. It would certainly appear to be unconscionable to use custody and access determinations as forms of punishment or compensation for any party. Except where abuse or neglect of children by either party is an issue, the parental rights (and the rights of children to both of their parents) should not be jeopardised under any circumstances.

The Family Law Act and the Court have established a number of principles for dealing with questions of maintenance after divorce that take account of the capacities of parties to support themselves, their ages and health, difficulties in re-entering the labour market after years of home production, responsibilities and costs arising from the custody of dependent children, and so on. Subject to the above, the Court holds that there is nevertheless a presumption that spouses have an obligation to support themselves as far as possible. There is no reason why these principles and presumptions should be changed, except by **adding**, to the fair entitlements so arrived at, an amount of financial and/or property compensation attributable to the damages (psychic, material or physical) inflicted on an innocent partner by the breach of contract.

Unilateral Divorce as Prima Facie Desertion

Consistent with the position being taken here, a unilateral petition for divorce in which the petitioner intends to lay no charge of breach of contract on the other partner at the divorce settlement should be taken as a prima facie act of marital desertion by the petitioner, thus leaving it open to the non-petitioning partner to claim damages for desertion, if he or she so wishes, at the divorce settlement. In circumstances where both parties allege breach of contract, it would be up to the Court to assess degrees of culpability and to apportion damages, if any, accordingly.

Implementing the Principles: A Hypothetical Illustration

Consider two hypothetical cases of two married couples, each with two children.

In the first case, the husband owns all the property and is the only source of family income. He fully maintains his wife and children, but treats his wife cruelly while caring adequately for the children. The wife applies for a divorce and when it comes to settling the terms of the divorce the wife accuses the husband of cruelty to her and proves her case. What should be the Court's response?

I have already argued that custody should go to a competent, non-abusing mother and access for one third of each year to a competent, non-abusing father. This is the case here, so the Court decides accordingly. Since the husband is clearly in default of the marriage contract and has damaged his wife and her interests in the marriage, the Court should award compensation in the form of property and financial settlements to the wife, over and above requiring the husband to continue providing maintenance for his former wife and the children.

In the second case, the wife petitions for divorce without accusing the husband of fault as a prelude to the divorce settlement, but the husband accuses the wife of adultery and proves it. The wife has no income or property of her own; all the marital property is jointly owned and she has been fully supported by her husband. What should the Court do? What kind of damages, if any, are appropriate?

Here, too, the custody and access arrangements I have suggested should prevail. Neither parent is incompetent or abusing, so the Court puts the children in the custody of the mother and the father has access to them for at least one third of each year. But is there any point in the Court awarding damages against the wife, who has virtually no capacity to pay? Is the husband to be doubly punished, in a sense, by the Court requiring him to support his children (who will leave his home) and an unfaithful wife?

The position is that the wife has forfeited her claim to maintenance by the husband, that she has damaged his legitimate marital interests and expectations, and that, in principle, he is owed compensation by her. But financial and property damages awarded against her would clearly prejudice her capacity to look after the children. The wife has freely chosen her course of action, in the absence of fault or intimidation by the husband, and ought to be prepared, therefore, to face the consequences of that choice. On the other side, the father cannot withdraw from his obligations to support the children and to share their guardianship. I would suggest that the Court should:

- formally award unspecified damages in favour of the husband;
- require the husband to pay continuing maintenance for the support of the children only, at a level that assumes that the mother will be responsible for accommodating them and looking after them

(unless the couple come to a consent agreement in these matters without requiring the court to make a determination);

- place all property acquired since the start of the marriage under the control of the husband, but without the power to dispose of it unless authorised by the Court, before the lapse of a certain minimum period (or, if this hypothetical situation were to be reversed in its particulars, under the control of the wife; i.e. whoever the 'innocent' party might be); and

- place no requirement upon the husband to pay maintenance for the wife, unless they had reached a consensual agreement otherwise.

Justice, or the Best Interests of the Children?

It might be suggested that a Court determination along these lines would unduly penalise the wife and might not be in the best interests of the children because there is no guarantee that the wife would receive voluntary maintenance from her former husband sufficient to enable her to provide care and housing for the children comparable to what they enjoyed in the formerly intact family. On the other hand, the father has already been required to provide at least the statutory minimum maintenance payments for the children. I therefore believe that it would be unfair for the Court to **require** the father, in addition, to maintain a contract-breaking spouse on the ground that this would seem to be in the interests of the children. In other words, in this case, the interests of the children should yield to the interests of justice and a more distant view of where the 'interests of children' really lie — whether in parental or in judicial discretion when there is no evidence that the parents are not caring and conscientious. So, it should be left to the father to decide what, if anything, he will do in addition to what the law requires him to do.

My view is that, beyond minimum, clear and just statutory safeguards, the best interests of the children should be left in the hands of non-abusing and competent — even though divorcing — parents to decide. It does not follow that a divorce renders parents insensitive to the interests of their children if they are protective of those interests while married; accordingly, the welfare of the children should not **drive** a divorce settlement, but should be annexed to the delivery of just treatment to the partners. Divorcing parents who believe that they have been dealt with fairly by the Court in relation to their marital affairs are more likely to deal rationally and objectively with decisions about the best arrangements for their children. Otherwise, they are likely to treat negotiations about the children as an occasion on which to be bloody-minded and unreasonable, in reaction to what they believe to be unjust and arbitrary treatment of their marital relationship. We also believe that these considerations would have the by-product (but not the intention) of enhancing the possibilities of reconciliation between the partners when the issues have been fairly judged and determined and when the various costs of divorce are fairly distributed and clearly seen.

A judgment along the lines sketched above might also be said to leave too much financial and property power, as well as discretion, in the hands of the 'innocent' partner (husband or wife, as the case may be). To this objection the only answer is that the deserting partner has not been driven away but has voluntarily forfeited claims to the joint exercise of that power and must live with the consequences of that decision; just as a partner to a commercial contract who unilaterally abandons it has no fixed claim to the property in the name of the partnership. Marital law reflecting such principles would be an example of the potentially valuable tutorial and moral functions served by certainty and predictability in the law when knowledge of the consequences of courses of action is available to the parties contemplating such action.

Certainty, Discretion and Fairness

The variety and complexity of the relationships in marriage, and the difficulties of establishing 'the truth' about subtle and intimate transactions of many kinds, inevitably create tensions between the delivery of both certainty and fairness under family law. Clear and definite rules may be certain, but their straightforward application might be felt to be unfair in certain circumstances. This difficulty must be acknowledged and it is not easily resolved. It is a matter on which the most practised and acute judicial minds might easily disagree. It is a difficulty recognised by the Courts themselves; by the Full Court of the Family Court in dealing with appeals against exercises of discretion by judges of first instance, and again when litigants appeal to the High Court against judgements of the Full Court of the Family Court.

For instance, in a recent paper The Honourable Justice Peter Nygh examines 'the role of the Full Court of the Family Court of Australia in guiding the exercise of discretion by judges at first instance' (1992:495). A major subject of his discussion is the struggle by the Family Court and its judges to maintain consistency (and hence certainty) in the face of the high degree of discretion afforded by the Family Law Act to individual judges. In an attempt to meet the problem, the Full Court of the Family Court has sought to enunciate various 'guidelines' for the edification of judges of first instance; for example, that in property disputes, 'equality should be considered the normal starting point' (1992:498). Yet, as Justice Nygh makes clear, the High Court has said that it cannot accept such guidelines as having the force of 'rules of law', and he adds that: 'In particular, the majority of the High Court expressly disapproved of decisions of the Full Court of the Family Court which had purported to apply equality as a starting point' (1992:498-9). In effect, the High Court reaffirmed the primacy of the discretionary power and the intention of the Parliament that this should be the case. In other words, no presumption of equality as a starting point is authorised by the Act.

Yet Justices of both the Full Court of the Family Court and of the High Court continue to concern themselves with the tension between on the one hand the need for consistency and certainty of the law and on the other hand the existence of wide discretion under the Act. In commenting on some remarks by Justice Deane of the High Court, Justice Nygh says:

> Thus his Honour is very conscious of the importance, desirability and even inevitability of 'general consistency' from one case to another of such underlying notions of what is just and appropriate in particular circumstances. According to his Honour such general consistency conforms with the ideal of justice in the individual case. Otherwise, he cautions — '. . . the law would in truth, be but "lawless science" and a "codeless myriad of precedent" and a "wilderness of single instances". . .' (1992:502-3).

It seems, then, that until the Parliament specifies what it understands marriage and its rights and obligations to be, a responsibility thoroughly fudged in the present Family Law Act, the Courts will continue to be denied the opportunity of dispensing consistent justice. In drafting a revised Act, the Parliament would be in a position to draw upon the accumulated wisdom of the courts and their practitioners in the light of their experience of the present regime.

I wish to emphasise, then, that the Act does not deliver marital justice and that it sacrifices too much in the way of certainty. In doing so, it creates behavioural consequences that undermine marital relationships and behaviour.

Summary

The discussion thus far leads to the following five conclusions:

(i) Marriage, if it is to have any real substance as an institution and way of life distinguishable from male-female cohabitation, must be seen as constituted by voluntary offering of vows and submission to contract.

(ii) Marriage and divorce law, if it is to support this conception of marriage, must provide sanctions for contract-breaking behaviour.

(iii) Divorce by consensus, or on the petition of one partner, must always be a right available for exercise, irrespective of the marital conduct of the parties.

(iv) Issues of justice arising out of the collision of (ii) and (iii) should be reconciled by punishing marital misconduct, if proven, through judicial determinations of compensation in settling the terms of the divorce.

(v) The present uncertainty and undue exercise of judicial discretion arising from the Family Law Act 1975 can be remedied by the adoption of clear principles consistent with the conception of marriage and divorce rights, and misconduct, detailed here.

The changes being proposed here are designed to solve, fairly, the impasse in which family law presently finds itself. The impasse arose from the desire to sever the granting of divorce from enquiry into the marital conduct of the partners. The important issue, it was thought, was not conduct but whether the marriage had broken down 'irretrievably' and, if so demonstrated by one year's separation, to make exit from it quick and simple. Questions concerning the reasons for the breakdown or of the moral conduct of the partners were simply irrelevant to that central issue of fact. Although this made consensual divorce easier and less painful, the upshot has been a system in which unilateral repudiation has been permitted without any consideration of the harm it might inflict or its unfairness. But so long as men and women believe that they have legitimate expectations about certain basic features of their partner's conduct in marriage, they will continue to believe that they have been unjustly treated if the law ignores default, the destruction of their married life and all that has been invested in it, because of misconduct by the other partner. That is the heart of the present impasse; and it is compounded by the present uncertainties attending questions of custody, property and maintenance.

Ironically enough, 'fault' is sometimes re-introduced through the back door when judgments about 'the best interests' of children in custody disputes are made in terms of the behaviour and capacities of the contending parents, the 'defaulting' parent, in such cases, being punished by denial of custody or restriction of access for behaviour that the law says (rightly or wrongly) is irrelevant to the custodial capacities of the parent concerned. Thus Finlay notes (1989:228):

> Sometimes a party's adulterous behaviour has been weighed against that party in a custody contest, **not because of moral turpitude** [emphasis added], but on the basis that the conduct has been disruptive of the marriage relationship. That being so, the argument runs, without wishing to punish the adulterous party for the adultery, it is regarded as more equitable [!] that the 'innocent' party should not be 'punished' in this way by being deprived of the custody of the child.

Nothing better illustrates the confusion, illogicality and arbitrariness engendered by the Family Law Act and the judicial discretion it promotes.

The impasse can be resolved only by restoring justice as a consideration that may be raised in divorce proceedings, while preserving the principle of 'unstoppable exit' by either unilateral or joint petition. Conduct becomes relevant only if one or both parties ask the Court to adjudicate alleged misconduct and, if proven, to make provision for compensation under the terms of a divorce which **must** be granted, irrespective of the conduct findings.

Chapter 6

Some Likely Consequences
of Family Law Reform

I f the Family Law Act were amended in these directions for reasons of justice alone, many valuable consequences would follow. Not least among these is the restoration of respect for the law. When a substantial body of law such as family law is perceived to be less interested in justice than in establishing procedural ease in sweeping away a failed marriage, its indifference to the plight of those who believe they have been ill-used or abandoned cannot help but provoke contempt, if not fury.

The rule of law is fundamental to our liberties and to the delivery of justice to all citizens. The freedom to make conscionable contracts and to be able to depend upon the law to uphold them or to provide compensations for default is an inextricable part of such a system and enjoys the widest public support. If the simple plea of this study is correct — that marriage is a contractual relationship or it is nothing in particular — then family law as it stands directly flouts the most elementary requirements of justice in marriage because it stands by helplessly as contractual abandonment runs rife without clear and predictable remedy.

The repair of marriage law is urgent for its own sake; but it is also a necessary aspect of maintaining respect for the law in general, and securing confidence in institutions and the behaviour of others. Good law is the friend of civil decency and personal responsibility.

Behavioural Effects

If family law were to be changed by allowing the right to sue for compensation for a broken marriage contract at the divorce settlement, this would have profound effects on the interwoven and complex structure of incentives and guarantees that promote trust and predictability in married life and largely determine whether couples will stay together or break up. Under a reformed Family Law Act, a partner contemplating desertion or infidelity or any other form of serious marital misconduct would be aware that such misconduct might incur penalties at a divorce settlement should the other partner choose to seek them. This would clearly influence his or her actual conduct.

If, as is sometimes the case, neither partner is guilty of serious misconduct but each finds it impossible to get on with the other, there is no obstacle to consensual divorce. But if a unilateral petition for divorce is to be treated, under revised law, as prima facie an act of desertion exposing the petitioner to a damages action by the other partner at the divorce settlement, there are two possibilities. The partner either will want desperately to end the marriage, and so will persist with the petition and be prepared to accept the consequences; or he or she will think again and 'try to make a go of it'.

Under the influence of a revised and **just** marital and family law, marital behaviour would become more considered and responsible and the functions the marital contract are intended to serve would be more likely to be realised.

Proving Fault and the Divorce Settlement

The reader who thus far broadly accepts the principles underlying the conception of marriage and divorce expressed here may nevertheless have reservations about the implications for husband-wife contests in court when the divorce and the terms of the settlement are not consensual. We have opened up the possibility of claims for damages for broken contract — claims that will have to be adjudicated. If the accused party contests the claim of default and compensation for damage, will we not return to the situation where proving 'faults' — adultery, cruelty, habitual intoxication, abuse and neglect of children, or such other contract-breaking actions as may be written into a reformed Family Law Act — re-introduces the whole process of presenting and examining evidence from private investigators, friends, neighbours, films, photos, records and documents before the Court?

There is some truth in this, but we should note a very important difference. It must be remembered that the Court contests, with sometimes lurid presentations of evidence of adultery, cruelty, drunkenness, and so on, that characterised some divorce petitions before the passage of the Family Law Act 1975 **were necessary in order to win the granting of a divorce**. Those circumstances encouraged their own distinctive set of motives. Under the reforms proposed here, there would be no return to that situation because such faults would not be **grounds** for divorce. Under my proposals, the divorce **must** be granted to a petitioner who submits a petition, irrespective of the marital circumstances and there is no **necessary** enquiry into whether the petitioner or his/her partner has been at 'fault'; the divorce must simply go ahead and no evidence is relevant to **that** outcome.

The only circumstances where evidence of 'fault' would be relevant and evidence taken by the Court is in winding up the marriage at the divorce settlement in circumstances where one or both of the parties wish to pursue an action for damages for breach of the marriage contract. If fault is proved, all that remains is for the Court to assess and award damages, or if fault is not proved, to make a judgment accordingly. But in either case the divorce goes ahead.

The necessity for taking evidence as to breach and damages is unavoidable if the marriage contract is to be taken seriously and justice offered to those who have been damaged by the breaking of it. To argue otherwise is to imply that marriage contracts are less important than, say, a rental lease or any other commercial contract. Yet we accept routinely that sorting out breaches of commercial contracts must be undertaken; otherwise injustice will be done and commerce will break down. Tedious though it might be, an offended party must have an avenue of legal redress no less in marriage than in other spheres where derelictions of freely undertaken obligations and abuses of rights occur.

In practice, it is unlikely that there would be many instances where accusations, entailing the possibility of costly proceedings, would be made lightly, especially if the Court were to follow the practice of awarding costs against an unsuccessful accuser. And there would, of course, be no restrictions on the parties, in seeking to adjust their differences, reaching compromises and settlements without resorting to litigation. The availability of recourse to the Court for damages for breach of contract would be a powerful incentive to reaching fair settlements. In the great majority of cases, it is likely that the resources of the Court in settling damages claims would be used only for those with serious, unresolvable and justifiable grievances. And they deserve the right to make their claim.

Underlying some objections to the 'washing of dirty linen' in court is a view of privacy which, while it is generous towards those involved and sympathetic to the actors in the human tragedy being played out, seeks to protect them from a public spectacle at the expense of larger issues. The delivery of justice to those actors is one of the issues, but the other is the long-term benefit to all that flows from the instruction to be gained from the open drama of justice in action as it wrestles with moral issues that go to the heart of living together. Only long-term good can come from public interest in (even though some of it might be prurient), and public discussion of, questions of behaviour and justice in marital and family relations. To focus minds upon such things, upon the moral and legal dilemmas and puzzles they throw up and the way the courts deal with them, and publicly and privately to discuss them, cannot help but contribute to better-informed, reflective, and discriminating citizens aware of the character of their society and its problems. This is important for a vigorous and open democracy. Not only does justice require the opportunity to prove damage in court, but the public interest requires that its delivery should be a process open to inspection and available for instruction, save where doing so might be contrary to the interests of any children involved in particular cases.

Marital Rights and Family Solidarity

The changes in the Act being recommended here would protect the contractual rights of the parties and preserve the option of divorce, while significantly reducing the incentives to act capriciously or selfishly in the marriage relationship. It would encourage responsible and fair behaviour and, **simply by doing that**, would tend to enhance the stability of marriage and family life, even though that is not the **intention** of the changes or their rationale.

The kind of stability that is relevant to us here is that evident in the coherent and predictable-in-principle behaviour which arises from conformity to broad behavioural guidelines known to all participants in advance, but which still allows considerable scope for individual initiatives. When the contractual guidelines of marriage are clear and enforceable, stability is a more common by-product. This is an example of the way good law in general works to ensure broadly predictable, stable, rule-governed behaviour when the rules are known to the participants and impartially applied. Just law enables the anticipation and avoidance of many potential points of conflict and instability and provides avenues for fair mutual adjustments and compromises in personal relationships. When stability occurs for these reasons, energies are diverted from potentially conflictual and possibly destructive outlets into more constructive ones, and families themselves and the rest of society are the beneficiaries. There can be little doubt that, in general, marital stability is good for the partners. Many studies show a clear correlation between good health and steady marriages and between bad health and divorce. The interests of children and their effective rearing are well served by stable families and, in consequence, the rest of society benefits from the more effectively socialised and moralised children that are more likely to emerge from intact families than broken ones.

But although the stability so engendered in marriages might also serve the interests of the wider community, it is not in itself a justification of the amendment of the rules of marriage and divorce I am proposing. It does not follow, from the greater stability and benefits that come from clear, fair and impartially-enforced rules, that the focus of family policy should be to ensure family stability at all costs. Such an approach is always in danger of coming to regard families as instruments for interests separate from the interests of families themselves, and that is a course fraught with potential for unintended consequences and counterproductive results. The focus should be to treat marital relations justly, and family circumstances fairly, and await the consequences.

The success of marriages or the well-being of families is not constituted or defined by the effectiveness of their service to the state, or 'society', or 'church', or 'party', or to any collectivity outside themselves, even though family members might, in fact, find their own deepest satisfactions and fulfilments in such service. The point is that a couple or a family, as such, does not depend for its meaning or value upon subservience to ends defined by others. From the point of view of public policy, they should be regarded as sufficient unto themselves.

Conclusion to Part One

The overall intention of this study is to go beyond the law of marriage and divorce dealt with in Part One and to consider, also, those other major elements of public policy that affect the well-being of Australian families in the widest sense. Family well-being involves much more than questions of family law.

But these wider issues cannot sensibly be discussed until we have first developed a sound basis for the legal status of marriage and divorce. The latter is too important, too fundamental to the formation of families and to their subsequent fortunes, to be left unexamined. The conditions of the legal integrity of families is a question **prior** to issues of their economic viability, their taxation status, and their capacity to care effectively for their children. A family system lacking the friendship of the law is handicapped from the beginning and its integrity is constantly under threat. That is a problem not only for individual families that will be less able to bear those shocks that are inseparable from the human condition, but also for the society that has to contend with family conflict and the consequences of breakdown.

Part One completes the discussion of those principles of reform of marriage and divorce law that I believe should underlie a revision of the Family Law Act. These reforms fall into two parts: first, the injection of more certainty and less judicial discretion in matters of property, maintenance, custody and access; and second, the serious reinstatement and affirmation of the contractual character of marriage. Both are important, but the second is the more fundamental. Family life cannot be securely based and the family be expected to serve its functions without the cooperation and support of the law **for those who voluntarily wish to marry (as distinct from cohabit) and form families**. This means that marriage, with its presumption of permanence and its public exchange of promises of mutual care and service, must be taken seriously as a contract and contract-breaking behaviour effectively penalised.

In view of the unavoidable moral-educative effects of the law, if the law takes marriage rights and obligations seriously and justly enforces them, so will wives and husbands take them seriously, and this cannot help but lead to more responsible and considerate behaviour. That is the foundation upon which reform in other areas impinging upon the well-being of families must be based. But marriages will still fail, and the preservation of an avenue of free and just exit is a liberty, complementary to the requirements of the marriage contract, that achieves that judicious balance of rights and obligations to which I referred at the outset.

If, then, we are to deal resolutely with the failures of the Family Law Act, some of which have recently been under examination by a Parliamentary Joint Committee, it is my contention that the conclusions of Part One of this study are essential components of any worthwhile movement for reform that might arise from that Committee's findings.

More broadly, for our further purposes here, Part One is the essential prelude to a consideration of the future of the Australian family in the context of a faltering economy and the 'welfare state'.

PART TWO

Work,
Welfare
and
Family
Taxation

Chapter 7

Employment, Unemployment And Welfare Dependency

A family, given the legal-contractual status for which I have argued, may be thought of as a continuous voluntary association of a particularly intimate and multi-faceted kind — a living, working microcosm that, particularly if dependent children are involved, strives to maintain itself and to serve the interests of its members. A generation or two ago, that would have seemed an obvious enough observation. But less so today. We tend now to see families as less cohesive, more fragile, more contingent, more exposed to outside forces and much less the mutual-welfare and supporting units they used to be. This has implications for the moral character of families. Their internal characters and those of their members are shaped not only by the law but by the **ways** in which they support themselves and by the extent to which the surrounding society encourages or discourages their efforts to be independent.

Marriages and families must subsist and seek their independence **in** society and cannot happily do so in hostile territory. In Part Two of this study, I shall be concerned with questioning whether public policy is conducive or hostile to family aspirations and independence. I argue that the two main requirements for this, in addition to just family law, are work and fair taxation. But meeting those requirements under present conditions and public policies is becoming increasingly problematic. We cannot avoid exploring why this is so and what the implications are. In this chapter and the succeeding one I discuss the importance of work for individual well-being and identity, the problems of **access** to work in contemporary Australia, the reasons for it, and its significance for welfare problems and the taxation burden being placed upon families.

Work and Identity

For the mass of mankind, work and family lie at the core of purpose and fulfilment in life. For all workers, men and women alike, work of all kinds and its connection to social roles, responsibility, self-esteem and independence, is central to dignity and identity. There are few circumstances that strike so deeply and profoundly at the core of personality and social participation as the loss of work, the denigration of one's work, or exclusion from work altogether. The availability of work and the rewards that come from it are largely determined, in Australia, by the interaction of industry protection, labour-market regulation, the welfare system and the taxation system.

There is a cruel contradiction at the heart of Australian welfare policy. One of its premises is that adults have a duty to work to support themselves if they can. It follows that it would be wrong for public policy to connive in denying men and women the opportunity of working or to create incentives to discourage them from working. Yet, in fact, we retain policies that do exactly this. This arises from the interaction in Australia between labour-market and wages regulation, tariff protection, welfare payments and 'poverty traps'. These relationships have been analysed in a contribution to the CIS Social Welfare Research Program by P.A. McGavin (1992). Since their interaction (the 'failing symbiosis', as McGavin puts it) has profound effects upon family welfare and morale, his basic argument deserves summarising for our purposes.

Behind tariff walls, and with the cooperation of the wages regulations of industrial-relations commissions and governments, Australia was able to establish a system of relatively high wages, restrictive practices and award rigidities that would have been unsustainable without protection from international and domestic market forces. But, over time, the high level of wages **for the employed** has increasingly made it difficult for those seeking work, especially the unskilled and poorly educated, to find employment because their low productivity and the legal requirement for high minimum (award) wages has made it uneconomic for employers to engage them. So the level of unemployment has risen, in conjunction with the substitution of machinery and electronics for expensive labour, especially in those sectors of the economy (e.g. mining and agriculture) exposed to international competition. The policy response to this, with the endorsement and encouragement of the union movement, has been to disarm protest by providing welfare payments to those who cannot find work. This has had two consequences of great economic and welfare importance. First, the nation has lost the productive potential of those who are not working, and second, the burden of funding welfare benefits for the growing numbers of unemployed and their families has put an ever-increasing taxation burden on those who remain in employment, and on the economy generally, that has further depressed the capacity of the economy to sustain the system. As McGavin puts it (1992:2–3):

Earlier Australian experience of high growth in *per capita* incomes and employment (as occurred during the 1960s, for example) meant that there was little scrutiny of the mutual dependence between the welfare state and market production and employment. The relationship between the two was not widely understood; they were assumed to be mutually beneficial. This was reflected in the union movement's support during the 1970s for the expansion of welfare-state provisions.

This relationship of mutual dependence is now more widely understood as **failing**.

Evidence of the failure is shown not only in the rising rate of unemployment, especially in youth unemployment and long-term unemployment among older workers, but in stagnant or falling real wages and rising taxation for the employed.

The Failing System

By the 1970s, as McGavin suggests, the failure of the 'symbiosis' was beginning to be revealed in the emergence of several inter-related trends. Wages grew rapidly, inflation accelerated into double figures, welfare spending expanded rapidly as payments for old-age pensions grew and, as the sole-parents' pension was introduced, payments for the increasing numbers of divorced and ex-nuptial mothers soared. At the same time, the age of full employment ended as high levels of unemployment became entrenched and, more recently, as youth unemployment became extremely high and intractable in association with the growth of long-term unemployment amongst older workers. Simultaneously, 'bracket creep' and rising levels of effective taxation began biting into disposable incomes, especially of families with a single income and dependent children.

Yet another phenomenon marking the discontinuities with the past and paralleling the general increase in unemployment was (as illustrated in Figure 2) the rapid growth of female employment — mostly part-time — which began to outstrip the growth in male employment (EPAC, 1992). This displacement of male employment by female employment, especially by female part-time employment, according to economist Alan Wood (*The Weekend Australian*, 11–12 July 1992), may be due to 'the response of employers to the rigidities imposed on the labour market by the complex and completely inappropriate structure of award wages and union monopoly practices'.

Wood may well be correct. If he is, then the trend will continue

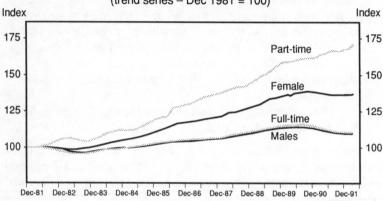

Figure 2
Employment growth in Australia
(trend series – Dec 1981 = 100)

Source: The Sydney Institute, *Commercial Issues* 10, 1992

so long as these rigidities — the outcome of a highly regulated and centrally-dominated labour market designed by men — persist in pricing men out of jobs — permanently.

An important thread in the impasse woven by the interconnections between wages rigidities and unemployment has been pointed out by Professor Bob Gregory (1992). He shows that in comparison with the United States, for example, our relative unemployment rate increased significantly in the 1970s in conjunction with substantial relative increases in Australian real wages (Figure 3). Gregory concludes that high levels of unemployment will remain unless there is a very significant fall (of about 35 per cent) in average real wages. Alternatively, the gap might be filled by very much higher increases in productivity, given the reforms of the labour market and other reforms necessary to stimulate them. Until then, we have to live with the situation summarised by Gregory (1992:41):

> Australia has quite clearly moved into a situation where average real wages have not significantly grown for fifteen years, part-time employment at low weekly earnings is being substituted for full-time work and within full-time work there is substitution of low weekly earnings for middle level jobs.

The drift of Professor Gregory's analysis is reinforced by Professor Judith Sloan of the National Institute of Labour Studies. She has estimated (1992) that under present circumstances the number of long-

Figure 3
Relative employment and real wages, US and Australia 1950–90

Source: Gregory, 1992

term unemployed could rise as high as 500 000 by the mid–1990s compared with 50 000 in 1978. She partly blames cyclical and structural changes for this but identifies the main cause as workers being paid 'in excess of market-clearing levels'. Exacerbating these artificially high, direct wage costs are the excessive extra costs, or 'on-costs', for such things as workers' compensation payments, payroll tax, leave loadings, superannuation, various allowances, and so on, which may add 50 per cent or more to direct wage costs.

Professor Sloan joins many other analysts who emphasise the crucial part played by artificially high wages, above market-clearing levels, and high on-costs, in causing and perpetuating high levels of unemployment, not only among young people (currently experiencing unemployment levels of more than 30 per cent), but also among older, unskilled workers and minority groups, particularly aborigines. In our early history, which parallels similar circumstances in the US, the high road to a better life for disadvantaged groups in society has been access to work through wage competition; competition that puts a high cost on employers who might wish to discriminate against such groups. It has also been one of the routes into the workforce of females, in earlier years. Such wage competition has been the means of access to on-the-job training and therefore of progression to more skilled, more highly paid occupations, by the disadvantaged. When relative wages are set by competition, employers can more easily afford to take on the unskilled and train them because their lower wages offset the costs of training.

The benefits of eliminating or reducing minimum wages are supported by overseas data. Max Walsh quotes American figures showing that 'The US experience of a low minimum wage regime has, on the face of the most obvious statistic, been outstandingly successful' (*The Sydney Morning Herald*, 16 July 1992).

In Australia, our current wage-setting arrangements, which perpetuate exclusion from work and training, which discriminate against the unskilled and ill-educated, which deny them realistic opportunities for on-the-job training, and which then compound their demoralisation by the seductions of welfare dependency, must therefore be seen as the keystone that holds together a deeply institutionalised and pernicious system that has profound effects on family life in this country.

From the perspective of family welfare, one of the more disturbing aspects is the concurrent trend for the proportion of long-duration unemployed with dependants to grow, rising from 25 per cent in May 1981 to 34 per cent in May 1990 (McGavin, 1992:19).

To meet the steadily rising welfare bill not only for unemployment payments but for other welfare benefits, disposable family income has contracted accordingly. McGavin points out that 'The equivalent marginal rate of taxation for a family with two dependent children with a one-person wage income at average weekly earnings increased from about 25 per cent in 1968 to 40 per cent in 1988' (1992:4).

So more and more people are being forced into unemployment, more of them are men and women with dependants and, for those who are employed, more and more of their income is being taken to provide welfare payments for those who are denied the opportunity to support themselves. The rising ratio of employment to dependency is shown in Table 2.

If it is wrong to deny men and women the opportunity of working at market-clearing wages, it is surely no less wrong to entice them to choose leisure over work, as we do when the rewards for working are vitiated by 'poverty traps' that make the income difference between unemployed welfare payments and (taxed) work-income negligible.

Most of the long-term unemployment is among those with few skills and therefore with low income-earning potential. This is the group — especially if married with dependants — whose total welfare payments most closely approximate the (low) incomes they would earn if employed. For example, an unemployed married man or woman with a non-working spouse and two dependent children aged 8 and 14 and getting rent assistance, would receive a family

Table 2
Employment, welfare dependency, and dependency ratio
for Australia, 1972 and 1984–90

Year	FTE-employment (millions)	Welfare recipients (millions)	Ratio of (b) to (a)	Dependency ratio (c), 1972 = 100
	(a)	(b)	(c)	(d)
1972	5.2	1.1	0.22	100
1984	5.8	2.7	0.46	214
1985	5.9	2.7	0.45	207
1986	6.1	2.7	0.44	203
1987	6.2	2.7	0.44	201
1988	6.6	2.7	0.40	185
1989	6.4	2.9	0.42	191
1990	6.8	2.9	0.43	198

Employment is full-time equivalent (FTE), and estimates are derived by dividing aggregate weekly hours worked (full-time and part-time) by average full-time weekly hours worked per person. These estimates are reported as four-quarter annual averages. Column (d) shows the dependency ratio at 1990 to be almost 200 per cent of the 1972 ratio. The calculation of 2.3 FTE employees to welfare dependents for 1990 is col. (a) divided by col. (b).

Sources: ABS, cat.no. 6203.0 and DSS, *Statistical Summary*, various issues, and computations on these data.

From McGavin, 1992:9.

income from the state of about $20 124.00 annually as at the date of writing. This is close to three quarters of the average adult full-time weekly earnings of employed persons ($589.20 per week) as at February, 1992 (ABS, 1992c). There is therefore only a weak incentive for such persons to seek work, given that an unskilled person would not be likely to receive the average wage if employed, but wages little different from the income from the state. They are seduced into the 'poverty trap' where unemployment benefits, with leisure, are preferred to low-paid work subject to high effective marginal tax rates when considered in relation to the loss or reduction of welfare benefits. Alan Tapper, in a valuable and succinct discussion of the creation and ramifications of poverty traps (1990a:141–47) cites research by the Brotherhood of St Laurence that indicates that a significant proportion of such people would forgo work rather than lose their benefits. One cannot blame those concerned for rationally and legally choosing what they believe is in their best interests. If there is a problem revealed here it arises from the mix of labour-market, welfare and taxation policies with which we began. The beginnings of a solution lie with changing them.

Unravelling the System

Although with some backsliding, and tenacious resistance from the privileged beneficiaries (including those enjoying protected and artificially high wages and the owners and managers of tariff-protected enterprises), there is now widespread political recognition that a crucial first step in beginning to unravel this destructive system is to expose the Australian economy to international competition by removing tariff barriers so that the real costs of the protection, in higher input costs and wages, are laid bare. This will be the basis for encouraging openness to competition, more realism and greater efficiency. The second step — although, ideally, it should be concurrent — is the removal of the restrictive practices and central-ised wage fixing that prevent individual enterprises from negotiating with employees and prospective employees to fix economically sustainable wages in a competitive labour market. The removal of minimum-wages legislation or substantial reduction in the minimum is central to achieving this, together with much stronger incentives to remove the temptation to choose leisure with welfare payments rather than work. Already there are appearing signs of labour market changes in response to recession, the beginnings of exposure to international competition, and attempts to escape the employment-stifling effects of excessive regulation and labour on-costs.

In concert with the changes noted by Professors Gregory and Sloan, casual, part-time and contract labour have grown substantially. This is clearly a move by industry to achieve greater labour flexibility and to minimise the rigidities and on-costs associated with full-time workers under centrally regulated industrial awards. In many cases, trade unions have cooperated in installing more efficient working methods in enterprises. But the key problems of general labour-market reform remain, in its centralisation, its on-costs, its wages regulation, and in the imposition of social objectives through indus-trial regulation in such matters as environmental protection, training, and superannuation. Strong opposition persists, with government support, to removing the array of regulatory and award impediments that prevent free wage negotiations over casual and part-time em-ployment. In short, what movement there has been is peripheral to the continuing opposition to core labour-market reform and genuine wages competition, without which industry will never fully recover its capacity to employ the million or so who languish in idleness and welfare dependency.

The Objectives and Costs of Reform

The links between the availability of work and labour-market reform, between welfare bills and high taxation, and between work, low taxation and family well-being are unmistakable. Employment-creating investment capital that might have been available from greater private saving under a less punitive taxation regime (necessary to pay the welfare bill), has not been available to create more jobs and higher real rates of pay under the more benign taxation that would then have been possible.

Inevitably, any significant unravelling of the mess will hurt those who have built their lives and expectations around arrangements that have grown up over many years. Yet the system is unsustainable without enormous waste, and the longer reform is delayed the greater will be the steady accumulation of decline and misery. It is important to remember that the decline is not simply **economic**; the economic outcomes simply reveal a deeper malaise whose origins are essentially moral and social.

Very often, the impulse behind the economic initiatives, however counterproductive the actual outcome, was a generous one or one based upon a conception of what was deemed to be just or fair, both in industrial matters and in society at large. But the system was also built upon a servile desire to be protected from reality and risk, no matter what the cost. It was built in large part upon the political search for privilege and unjustified advantage over others; upon protection from competition; upon a denial of equal opportunity; upon coercion and threat; upon the closure of the open society; upon endless regulation of more and more of the economy and daily life; upon loss of liberty; upon illusions and the subversion of the rule of law. All of these are the continuing costs of the system, over and above the economic costs, so long as we retain it.

The objectives of reform and the imperative of dispensing with illusions are clear even if the methods of achieving them are not. Just how difficult it is to undo the knots has been shown in recent debate over youth wages and especially the relationship between youth wages and (award) wages for adults. But the problem must somehow be solved, because this is the bedrock of labour-market reform without which all that employment and work means for the viability of marriage and family life and individual well-being will be lost and the family-damaging burden of taxation will remain. Family independence and well-being depend upon the availability of work and lower taxation, which in turn require reform of the labour-market and reduction in the welfare bill.

We will shortly return to the question of taxation and family independence when we consider the economics and politics of supporting and caring for children. The foregoing discussion is intended to place what comes later in the context of the connections between the costs of the welfare state, taxation, and the labour market.

Chapter 8

The Consequences Of Family Breakdown

The contraction of employment within a wage-inflexible labour market is one factor, of unknown significance, in the complex of factors involved in family breakdown and less-than-optimal family performance. The growing labour-force participation of women and their greater independence is another. But we do not know **how** important it is, nor do we know for sure **why** women work, although Mariah Evans's research (1989) suggests that the reasons are highly variable across different groups. And so it goes for the other factors that I mentioned earlier.

There is also a genuine issue raised by the question, 'Does it all matter?'. Is it not possible that we are too sentimental about 'the family' and, as some feminists might suggest, too uncritical of it? Might there not be more good than bad in men and women coming together and separating freely, as they wish? Does divorce or separation matter all that much? Aren't the effects on children exaggerated? To those questions, this study has a single response: What matters is the rights and duties of individuals and affected third parties in relation to marriage and family formation. We have already dealt with what that means in marriage and divorce. We need now to discuss what it means to children, and to citizens and taxpayers forcibly involved as affected third parties. An instance of the latter is the way in which sole parenthood impacts upon others not directly involved.

Sole-Parent Families

In addition to unemployment benefits, and old-age and invalid pensions, for which the 1991–92 federal budget set aside a total of more than $18 billion, a major item in the welfare bill that raises taxation for all, including intact families, is public support of sole parenthood, for which $2.924 billion in expenditure was budgeted for 1991–92.

Far and away the most important cause of sole parenthood is divorce, separation or desertion by married and de facto married partners. Unmarried motherhood accounts for about 3 per cent of sole parenthood but, as a percentage of births, ex-nuptial births have increased fivefold over the last 40 years.

In addition to the role to be played by labour-market reform, progress towards solving at least part of the problem of the costs, both social and financial, of sole parenthood depends upon three things:

less divorce, separation and desertion; removal of the monetary incentives provided by sole-parent pensions for marriage or de facto marriage breakups and ex-nuptial parenthood; and continuing refinement and effective enforcement of the Child Support Scheme (about which more below).

The Increasing Burden

The steady increase in broken families, ex-nuptial parenthood, and hence numbers on supporting parents pensions, is unprecedented in Australia but has much in common with recent experience in Britain and the US. In all three countries these trends are associated with easier divorce, more generous welfare benefits, unemployment, a taxation squeeze on intact families, greater workforce participation by wives and mothers, and greatly increased expenditure on the elderly.

In Australia in 1991 there were over half a million children in 383 500 sole-parent families, headed by women in 87 per cent of cases (ABS, 1991a). One birth in every five (almost 50 000 annually) is to an unmarried mother. The percentage of ex-nuptial births to total births is, at 22 per cent, five times the 1947 rate of 4 per cent. In 1986, 176 730 persons received supporting-parents pensions. Information supplied to the author by the Commonwealth Department of Social Security after telephone enquiry indicates that by May 1992 there were 285 774 recipients of this pension, comprising 269 593 females and 16 181 males. Of the female recipients, 51 844 were unmarried, but a 1984 survey by the Institute of Family Studies suggests that about half of these would have been involved in de facto marriage relationships. For the rest, the overwhelming majority of supporting parents were divorced or separated or had been deserted by their partners.

Some 87 per cent of sole parents are women. Divorce, separation or desertion for most women with dependent children, along with custody of those children, results in a sudden decline in income. But there is no reason to believe that such women, as a class, were any richer or poorer, worse or better educated, on average, **within** marriage or cohabitation, than the rest of the relevant population (Jordan, 1987). They are, in short, an average cross-section of the married or cohabiting female community with children. So why are they and their children now poorer in such a way as to merit public support? There appear to be two main reasons. First, a separated couple usually needs to support separate households entailing increased overhead costs and the loss of the former economic advantages of division of labour and cooperation. Given no increase in the partners' incomes following separation, and higher total costs, this disadvantage usually falls more heavily upon the woman. Second, the (usually) non-custodial male partner is likely to be the higher-income earner, he may more easily reduce his living costs in the absence of partner and child(ren), and he may evade his responsibility to provide maintenance.

The Child Support Scheme

By the late 1980s concern had emerged that children of separated parents were not receiving sufficient financial support from non-custodial parents. The Child Support Scheme was introduced by the Commonwealth in 1988, in two stages, and established a maintenance-collection agency, the Child Support Agency, as part of the Australian Taxation Office. Payments are collected, where practicable through automatic wage deductions, and passed over to the Department of Social Security for distribution to custodial parents. The Family Court formerly set levels of maintenance but in 1989 this function was taken over by the Child Support Agency.

Of the 265 709 sole-parent pensioners at 21 June 1991, some 103 064 (39 per cent) were declaring maintenance income. This represents a rise from the 26 per cent declaring maintenance before the Scheme began (Commonwealth Department of Social Security, 1991:134–6). This trend is represented in Figure 4.

The Scheme has therefore had some success in increasing the scope of maintenance payments, but it seems that a substantial majority (61 per cent at 21 June 1991) of non-custodial parents are not meeting their maintenance responsibilities. The bill is presented instead to the rest of the community, including intact families supporting their own children. Whether, and when, this is fair is a question that cannot be answered without enquiring into the faults and deserts of the formerly married or cohabiting partners.

Whose Problem Is It?

Consider four sorts of situation. In the first, a woman with one or more children has a husband who supports his family adequately, but she is so cruelly treated by him that she divorces him. No one would blame her, but the community might legitimately expect that the husband should continue to provide sufficient support for his former depend-ants to absolve the community from doing so. We might therefore

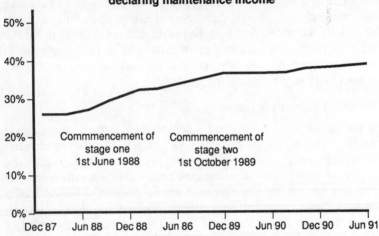

Figure 4
Proportion of sole parent pensioners
declaring maintenance income

Source: Dept. of Social Security, *Annual Report 1991*

expect the law to rigorously enforce such an obligation, and this it is trying to do through the Child Support Scheme with, so far, limited success.

In the second situation, a woman with a young child commits adultery and her husband, who has always supported them well, divorces her. Should society ignore the woman's behaviour and support her and her child? Is the husband under an obligation to do so?

In the third situation, a comfortably-off couple decide that they cannot live together, and consensually divorce. The woman and her children are now poverty-stricken. What should be the obligations of the man and woman and of the community?

In the fourth situation the husband deserts a 'blameless' woman and disappears without trace, leaving the woman destitute and with young children to support. Few would deny that woman's claim to aid.

To raise such questions takes us back to our earlier discussion about justice in marriage and divorce and the responsibilities and obligations to spouses and children that should go with it. The question of providing or withholding public aid for sole parents following separation, divorce and desertion cannot be isolated from the moral character of the actions of the parties that created the situation to be dealt with. If we do otherwise we inevitably inflict

injustices upon 'innocent' taxpayers who, in some cases, will effectively be put in the position of rewarding those who forfeit their
obligations and saving them from the consequences of their voluntary,
but reprehensible, actions. That is an excellent way of encouraging the
perpetuation of the actions in question.

Parents cannot absolve themselves of the obligation to support
their children by separating or divorcing, and public policy should
strenuously bend itself to ensure that this does not happen by evasion.
Broken or separated families, with the exception of those exposed to
unavoidable hardship through no fault of their own, have no entitlement to privileges bought at the expense of others. This is a matter we
will return to in the discussion of the care of children.

Economic Incentives, Ex-Nuptial Births and Sole Parenthood

Most women probably contemplate having at least one baby at some
stage in their reproductive years and would hope to do so without too
much hardship.

Apart from the act of fathering, men are important or unimportant
to this process in proportion to their capacity to reduce hardship. If the
presence of the father entails a significantly higher mother-child
income, the mother has an incentive to marry and stay with him;
otherwise he is more readily dispensable either before or after
marriage. Other things being equal, mothers with children, or women
thinking of having one, make an economic calculation and go where
the money is.

Nothing is more natural for most young women than to contemplate motherhood. If it attracts them and they can achieve it with the
guarantee that hardship will be reduced by support from the state, in
the absence of a guarantee of adequate support from the father or
another man, it will be more likely to happen; particularly if the young
woman has poor workforce skills, little prospect of employment, or
employment at a wage significantly above the supporting-parent
pension, and if no social stigma dissuades her from unmarried
motherhood.

This is not to say that such women will have ex-nuptial children
solely because of the supporting-parent pension, but only that its
presence removes an important disincentive (extreme economic hardship) to something that is otherwise to be regarded pleasantly as a form
of fulfilment for lives that might otherwise be sterile, in more senses
than one. As Charles Murray (1986:4) puts it, 'welfare does not **bribe**
poor women to have babies, it **enables** them to do so'.

A Case Study

Although by no means conclusive in this matter, a small-scale study carried out by Dr Ian Spencer (1992) in a New South Wales country town is consistent with the view put above. As a general practitioner in the town, he became aware of a large number of unmarried teenage pregnancies of which the majority were of girls in families suffering long-term unemployment. In no way critical of the girls or their actions, Spencer came to believe that 'with the very low education expectation, and job expectations, of these girls, their attitudes to realistically looking for careers in their early years other than mother-hood was very low' (*sic*). He also formed 'the firm opinion that the contraceptive knowledge within the group was really quite high'.

Spencer cautiously and properly acknowledges that his sample (drawn from more than one country town) is small, and that therefore the study is not statistically robust. However, he concludes:

> From a descriptive point of view, there did seem to be a common denominator of longstanding unemployment, low education profile and very low job expectation within these teenage girls, which made them look towards motherhood as a worthy and viable strategy for surviving into the 1990s.

To which we might add the reasonable inference (in view of the girls' contraceptive knowledge) that these were **deliberate** choices of ex-nuptial motherhood made against a background significantly changed by the availability of supporting-parent pensions; a background quite different, therefore, from the even more desperate unemployment environment of the 1930s depression when the rate of ex-nuptial births fell, and when there was no supporting-parent pension.

But it would be quite wrong to infer that ex-nuptial parenthood is predominantly a teenage phenomenon; quite the contrary. Adele Horin, reporting work by the welfare organisation Brotherhood of St Laurence, points out that the number of unmarried women in their thirties on sole parent pensions has risen 400 per cent in the last decade to 10 500, and that the number of teenage single mothers on the pension has remained stable at about 5000 for many years (*The Sydney Morning Herald*, 1 April 1992).

Married to the State

Today, a single mother with a child under 13, living away from the parental home and receiving full rent allowance, would receive a sole-parent pension and allowances totalling $237.15 each week. If living (unofficially) with an unemployed de facto husband receiving a jobsearch allowance of $105.90 per week, plus full rent assistance of $31.45 per week and income from other sources up to $60 per week, their combined annual income would be of the order of $22 586, or 86 per cent of the average weekly full-time adult earnings of employed persons, as at February 1992 (ABS, 1992c). Money makes a difference, especially for the poorly educated with poor employment prospects, even if the 'spouse' is the state.

Drawing on both Australian and American data, Peter Swan and Mikhail Bernstam conclude (1987:17), after a lengthy analysis, that 'the massive rise in welfare dependency relating to Supporting Parent Benefits is due to the long-term worsening of the employment market', and they remark elsewhere (1989:235) that:

> Finally, our work on single-parenting emphasises that reforms are needed in job markets at the same time that changes are made to social security programs. The number one priority is a more flexible labour market without award and minimum wage provisions. These are simply devices used to deny poorly-skilled workers access to jobs.

Unmarriageable Men

Professor Gregory notes that the huge loss of full-time employment over the last 20 years has been concentrated upon males: 'More than twenty-five per cent of male full-time employment, adjusted for population growth, has been lost since 1970'. He goes on to point out that 'there has been a continuing trend for men to withdraw from the labour force and to move on to government income support' (1992:14). So, young men, excluded from work by a highly regulated labour market, are denied the employment that might encourage them to contemplate supporting a family. They direct their attention elsewhere and drift into idleness and welfare dependency, or worse.

Or, if a married or de facto married couple experience marital or cohabiting problems, one way out may be divorce, separation or desertion in the knowledge that the state stands ready to provide support for the mother and child. Another possibility is that a proportion of these men may be persuaded by the availability of welfare support and paid leisure to cohabit (unofficially) with unmarried mothers on supporting parents' pensions and, in so doing as a couple, to jointly garner a tax-funded income from the state that is equivalent to that earned by a significant proportion of employed and taxpaying workers supporting one or more dependants.

Commenting on an uncannily similar trend of events in Britain, Patricia Morgan says (1989):

> As it is, benefits and tax reliefs for the children of broken marriages, or single mothers, put a premium on family breakdown, lone parenthood, de facto as opposed to legal marriage and the general casualisation of paternal responsibilities. It is effectively pricing bona fide husbands and fathers off the market.

Speaking for the United States, the President of the Family Research Council asks why young American mothers have ex-nuptial children and what happens to marriageable men under comparable American welfare arrangements. He answers as follows:

> Government offers the unmarried mother an attractive contractual arrangement: The equivalent of somewhere between $U.S.8,500 and $U.S.15,000 per year in combined welfare benefits, on condition that the young woman **not work for pay, and not marry an employed male**.

And as for marriageable men:

> The system makes them economically useless. Their potential role as husbands and custodial fathers is squeezed out by the government, so they seek other outlets for affirmation. (Bauer, 1992:4)

Sole parenthood will always be with us for a variety of reasons: death, divorce, misadventure, desertion, choice, perceived economic advantage, and so on. The reasons are nobody's business except those directly concerned, save in three circumstances: when the outcome of private decisions leads to a claim on other taxpayers that is difficult to justify; when public policy itself creates incentives to become public dependants; and when law and public policy lead to harm or injustice to third parties, such as children.

I have discussed some aspects of the first two outcomes and the interaction between economic circumstances, public policy and personal decision-making. It remains to consider the effects on children.

Chapter 9

Divorce, Sole Parenthood, and the Needs of Children

I t was earlier noted that child poverty is much more common in sole-parent families, with obvious consequences for child welfare in many cases. The poverty usually follows divorce, desertion and the avoidance of their maintenance obligations by ex-spouses, over-whelmingly men. I have also noted some evidence suggesting that poverty and lack of employment opportunities may itself be a contrib-uting factor to sole parenthood and dependence on the state. Austral-ian evidence on such connections is sparse, but there is English evidence that sole parenthood is more common in areas of high unemployment (Willetts, 1991:12).

One cannot argue, of course, that sole parenthood or poverty are always and necessarily bad for children; so much depends upon the actions and attitudes of the parents and there are clearly thousands of cases where mothers and fathers alone and in difficult circumstances have managed to rear their children well. But neither can it be denied that the presence of two loving and conscientious parents enjoying a reasonable income is the optimal child-rearing environment in most cases. Insofar as public policy provides incentives that encourage the formation of family arrangements that are sub-optimal for the rearing of children or which encourage the cavalier treatment of the interests of children, it is to be condemned.

A number of instances have been given of the ways in which family law, labour market, wages and employment policies, pensions for sole parents and ex-nuptial mothers, and evasions of maintenance obligations by non-custodial spouses frequently act against the welfare of children and hence the formation of 'human capital'. Children and their interests are one of the reasons, for example, why divorce involving children cannot be a purely private issue. Parents cannot divorce their children; they cannot escape their obligations through divorce. Having a child within a marriage immediately implicates a third party in the union who, without the protection of the law, would be voiceless in defending the interests that hang upon that union.

The Effects of Parental Separation on Children

Most books and articles that deal with divorce, family breakdown and out-of-home child care properly devote considerable space to the effects upon children and their development. For the reader who wishes to assess some of the evidence bearing on the conditions for well-functioning families and child development, an excellent Australian discussion is to be found in Moira Eastman's *Family: The Vital Factor* (1989). Alan Tapper's magisterial study (*The Family in the Welfare State*, 1990a) of most of the important aspects of family life and welfare under Australian conditions includes a discussion of some of the causes and consequences of family breakdown. There is a large body of research, mostly American and British, dealing with the relationships between child development, maternal care and out-of-home care; the significance of mother-child bonding; the effects of divorce on adults and children of varying ages; the development of children in sole-parent families; and related matters. Among the more prominent authors in the field are Jay Belsky (1986), John Bowlby (1982), Judith Wallerstein and Sandra Blakeslee (1989), Karl Zinsmeister (1988, 1992), and Ann Mitchell (1985).

It is not our intention here to go into this evidence in detail, but two things must be said about research in these areas. Not all of the evidence shows ill effects of divorce on children, nor do the early childhood studies show that out-of-home care is necessarily undesirable. As common sense would lead us to suspect, for some children the divorce of their parents is the lesser of two evils in releasing them from household purgatory and turmoil. For some very young children, high-quality day care of limited duration shows no ill effects and, for 3–5 year-olds, pre-school kindergarten is commonly an integral part of normal development.

So it all depends: on the nature of the pre-divorce and post-divorce circumstances; on the ages and personalities of the children; on the attitudes and actions of the parents; and, in respect of child care, on a whole host of factors to do with the age of the child, length of separation from parents (especially mothers), the degree of affectionate concern by carers, family relationships of substitute carers, and so on. Nevertheless, while we should acknowledge the need for caution and careful qualification, a balanced view cannot ignore a substantial body of disturbing evidence about the effects of divorce, sole parenting and out-of-home child care, under certain circumstances that are not uncommon.

In a recent review of the evidence, Karl Zinsmeister draws the following two conclusions. First, youths from single-parent or step families, in a study of 17 000 American children, were two to three times more likely to have had emotional or behavioural problems than those from intact families. Second, children from single-parent families were more likely to have low educational achievements.

As for out-of-home child care, he notes (1992:1003–04):

> No matter what the funding levels, the skills of the staff, or the motivation, the clear conclusion of child development clinicians — from Anna Freud to John Bowlby on up to the present — is literally that the most humdrum, average family typically does a far better job of rearing its young into well-adjusted and effective citizens than any enlightened group of professionals could in the family's breach.

In relation to divorce, research has not ignored the possibility that in some cases the ill-effects of divorce may be due to family circumstances that **pre-date** the divorce. A recently published longitudinal study by Cherlin et al. (1991) suggests that pre-existing family dysfunction and conflict may account for behavioural and educational problems among children of divorced parents and that the divorce may in fact have improved what was a child-damaging situation. However, after a detailed analysis of the methodology and circumstances of this study Richard Gill concludes that such an inference is not necessarily justified and draws attention, among other things, to the probability that 'a society in which there is an easily accessible and socially acceptable divorce option will also be a society in which family dysfunction and marital conflict will be more common' (1992:91).

British research on the effects of divorce and sole parenthood on children (Mitchell, 1985) is consistent with the adverse findings of the bulk of American studies and supports, also, the correlation of low educational achievement and crime with sole parenthood (Green, 1991:22).

Richard Gill, in the article referred to above (1992:81), refers to

> an accumulation of data showing that intact biological-parent families offer children very large advantages compared to any other family or non-family structure one can imagine. Not only are these advantages indisputable in economic terms, they are equally hard to contest where children's' emotional development, behaviour, health and school performance are concerned. If one had to select the single most important factor responsible for the disturbing condition of many of today's

younger generation — a condition that almost everyone views with alarm — the break-down of the intact biological-parent family would almost certainly be near the top of the list.

Families Without Fathers

One of the most interesting and forcefully argued of recent studies of the sources and anti-social effects of family breakdown, especially the effects upon the behaviour of youths, is *Families without Fatherhood*, by Norman Dennis and George Erdos (1992). The core of their work is an analysis of two large-scale British family studies, with particular reference to the effects upon children of 'committed' and 'uncommitted' (often absent) fathers. From about 1960 in England, they remark: 'The notable aspect of national life that has been dramatically changing at the same time as civil life has been deteriorating is the family. The change to which we direct particular attention is the progressive liberation of young men (partly at the insistence of women themselves) from the expectation that adulthood involves life-long responsibility for the well-being of their children' (1992:xxi).

Dennis and Erdos go on to dissect the findings of the studies referred to and their social-scientific significance in the light of recent academic studies of the family. They remark in passing: 'As a current sociological phenomenon, it is interesting that so much discussion is directed to, as we might term it, "explaining away" the findings that show that across the board, physical weight, height, educational achievements, criminality, life and death itself, are on average connected with the presence or absence of a committed father' (1992:44). And they finally conclude a little later: ' But it is pure obscurantism to deny that the statistical chances of children being physically smaller, stammering, being poor scorers in intelligence tests, or having a criminal record, depended greatly on their home background; and the quality of their home background, at the time of the Newcastle 1000 studies, depended greatly upon the father' (1992:58).

Conclusions

In the face of the evidence, three broad generalisations seem fair. First, divorce, separation and sole parenthood with 'uncommitted' fathers, are associated with a great deal of suffering and distress for many, probably most, children, and are frequently followed by serious emotional and behavioural problems, including criminality. Second, for the first two years of life, a baby's normal development may be threatened if it is denied close and constant contact with its mother.

Third, for very young children, out-of-home care is sub-optimal.

If we accept these generalisations, what are the implications for parenting, law and public policy, considered in the light of our earlier discussions? We have seen that family law and welfare policies may often have the unintended consequence of providing incentives for divorce or separation or, at least, of mitigating the disincentives. Much the same is true of ex-nuptial parenthood. Where this happens, public policy is directly implicated in damaging the interests of children in two ways. First, it contributes to the breakdown of families and parental separation with the bad effects on children that that commonly has. Second, by raising the taxation burden on intact families, it reduces the resources that would otherwise be available to them, and this directly affects family welfare and the well-being of their children.

In sum, current policy encourages irresponsibility, injustice, welfare dependency, and waste.

Apart from welfare policy, the present state of family law is a major cause of children being deprived of normal parental care and maintenance. Accordingly, our point of departure here is to reaffirm the primacy of justice in the marriage relationship and the obligations of parents to do their best for their children. If the law effectively enforces marital justice, there will be less ill-considered and ill-judged divorce and separation, and therefore fewer children facing parental separation and all that that implies. But when divorce is unavoidable, good parents, divorced or not, will want to do their best for their children and this is more likely if the partners can part under broadly predictable and just conditions.

Beyond this, no more can be done by parents than to inform themselves fully about, and to realistically face, what the best evidence shows as the consequences of divorce for themselves and their children. In this, as in other family matters, they should retain their autonomy and freedom of decision. If it is true that divorce is, on the whole, seriously disturbing for children, that is a factor in the equation that cannot be ignored. The facts should not be concealed or muted in the interests of self-delusion and should be taken into account as part of the duty of parents to their children. In other words, there is no role here (apart from the prevention of direct abuse) for public policy, only for private initiatives and self-education.

Much the same applies to parents' decisions about child-care arrangements. There are risks associated with separating a child from its mother for long periods in the first year of its life. Day care may not be harmless for children up to three years of age. If it is true, on the whole, that the best carers for young children, especially in the first year or two, are their own parents or close relatives, the implications of that for parental behaviour and choice should be faced. In this regard, public policy, as I shall be arguing in more detail later on, is totally unjustified in devising financial incentives (such as child-care subsidies favouring working mothers) or economic penalties designed to encourage or force mothers into the workforce against their wishes. Public policy should be neutral in the matter and choices must rest with the parents to make in accordance with their own needs and circumstances, and their own judgment.

Chapter 10

The Costs Of Children

In this chapter the issue of family taxation is discussed. We examine, in particular, the taxation status of children and the principles of family taxation that follow from this. The issue of child care is considered from two perspectives: fairness to all families, and the effective formation of human capital. But we begin by asking some questions about the social role of families and the obligations of the state, if any, towards the costs of rearing children.

Government Support for Child-Rearing Costs

Should the government give tax concessions or subsidies to help meet the costs of rearing children? Would the national interest be served or damaged if it were to do so? Would it be unfair to the childless? Is it simply a question of justice and equity? If there is a just claim, what is its basis and how should it be met?

The answers to these questions are of great importance for public policy. Yet, with one or two exceptions (Jordan, 1987; Tapper, 1990a) they have hardly been discussed in recent years as the actual level of **some** concessions and subsidies for parental child-rearing has declined, especially for middle-income families with dependent children and only one wage- or salary-earner. For example, although recently indexed to the Consumer Price Index, over the last nine or ten years the rebates for dependent spouses and children have fallen in real value by about 30 per cent and the family allowance (means-tested from 1987 and assets-tested from 1992) has fallen in real value by over 40 per cent.

When this reduced level of public support (except for sole-parent and low-income families) is combined with inflation and bracket creep from the early 1970s until 1991, with higher taxation and real-wage stagnation and decline, the median family finishes up paying more in taxes than it receives in benefits (Tapper, 1990a:113–15). It might be said that **some** families get subsidised child care which they did not get before — but more about that later.

Economic welfare and government support for many families with children has thus declined significantly. An important counterpoint to this has been **increased** funding for some family situations (e.g. sole-parent families, low-income families); for later stages in the life cycle (e.g. aged pensioners); for particular kinds of child-rearing costs (e.g. out-of-home child care); and steady growth in welfare payments generally, although somewhat constrained in recent years by economic and budgetary problems, as shown in Figure 5.

Why are we witnessing changing patterns of tax-funded expenditures on families and 'dependants', with some losers and some winners, within an overall environment of more comprehensive (and expensive) governmental concern for questions of 'welfare'? This question, and the questions with which we began, raise issues that go to the heart of the modern, highly regulated, redistributive, welfare state.

Family and State: The Changing Pattern

In the middle of the 19th century, the average family — very much poorer than today's — had six children and received virtually no help from the state. Today, the average family has fewer than two children, and although it receives a variety of exclusive 'benefits' in exchange for its taxes — such as subsidised Medicare cover for its dependent children, free education, child allowances — it still finishes up square or worse off. Matters that were formerly attended to by families out of their own resources and without interference are today brought within the purview of the state, which uses its taxing and regulatory powers more extensively to redistribute income and to provide subsidies and services under highly regulated conditions.

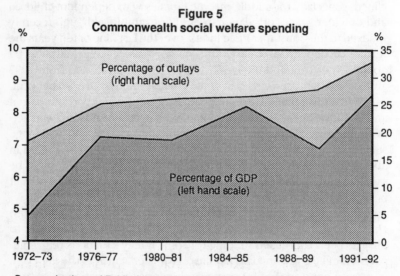

Figure 5
Commonwealth social welfare spending

Source: Institute of Public Affairs & 1991/92 Budget Papers

The relative harshness of life in the 19th century was essentially due to the much smaller per capita national income rather than to the absence of help from a very much smaller and relatively impoverished state. The independent family was the main support of society's 'dependants' — the very young, the old, the unemployed, the disabled, the sick — backed by a variety of voluntary associations, church groups, charities and the emerging friendly societies (Green, 1984).

The social and welfare history of the modern state is largely one of transferring responsibility for 'dependants' from private hands, especially families and other voluntary associations, to public hands, along with a consequent transfer of money, via taxation and redistribution, from private to public control. But it is more than that. An important consequence is that it also moves authority and decision-making from the private to the public arena, transforming social, economic, and therefore moral, relations. It establishes a different moral order, aptly summed up in the phrase 'the client state', in which formerly independent citizens and their workplaces become the welfare clients of multiple public bureaucracies and subjects of their regulations. As a result, the family, considered as a continuous economic unit, working and producing to support its members and often binding three generations in a cycle of dependency, work and dependency, has all but disappeared.

As a free, discriminating purchaser of education for its children in an educational market, family choice has been largely supplanted by tax-funded, state-determined-and-produced education (West, 1991a,b). For those unable to afford private education, options are highly restricted and so therefore is the parents' capacity to select and help shape their children's educational experiences. When interest groups attain inordinate influence within the bureaucracies that determine school curricula and texts, children become captive audiences for propaganda and falsehoods, as evidenced in mid–1992 by the notorious (and subsequently withdrawn) environmental 'information kit' *Give the World a Hand*, distributed by the federal Department of Arts, Sport, the Environment and Tourism.

The extension of schooling, unmatched (as many would argue) by a proportionate increase in knowledge or skills gained, has increased the economic burden of children and delayed the time when they might contribute to family finances. Many teenagers stay on in school, re-enrol in secondary school or enrol in tertiary education to avoid the unemployment that would otherwise await them. In the meantime, as we have seen, something like 30 per cent of those teenagers already in the labour market are denied employment.

Young adults still support the aged and the needy, but no longer in their own ways through their families or voluntary associations, but indirectly, and in accordance with state-determined criteria, through the tax system and the huge, impersonal apparatus of the state that breaks the moral nexus between the supporter and the supported.

The dominant pattern, then, of the last 100 years or so has been the steady attenuation of families' inter-generational bonds, their independence, their cooperative economic relations and their welfare, educational and mutual-insurance functions. Against such a background, minimally sketched here, it is not surprising that marriage and fertility rates should fall (Maley, 1990). It is also this background that colours our initial questions, because 100 years of state intervention has undermined the economic *raison d'être* of children as potential workers for the family and supporters of aged parents. When children performed these functions there was a stronger incentive for adults to have them. They were substantial 'private goods' within a self-sustaining system which, although it might also yield the public side benefit of delivering new citizens and producers for an ongoing society, required no public support or encouragement in order to yield that benefit. So, if that system has gone, if the private benefits of children to their parents now entail great economic costs and the virtual disappearance of off-setting economic benefits, the incentives for sustaining a volume of children sufficient to yield whatever might be the private and public benefits of children in general are greatly weakened.

The Case for Collective Support for Child-Rearing Costs

However, this does not mean that public recognition of the costs of child rearing and arguments for public support for parents depend upon demonstrating that children in general are good for society. Attractive as such an approach and such arguments might seem to be, they ultimately undermine the central principle of maximising family autonomy and avoiding public policies that violate what should be the neutrality of the state in relation to intra-family decision-making. Such arguments are difficult to sustain without making contestable political assumptions and, accordingly, they introduce potentially dangerous principles that legitimise government interference in family matters.

For example, some argue that governmental manipulation of rewards and punishments for parents to encourage high fertility, or moderate fertility, or zero-growth fertility, or falling fertility are desirable **population** policy objectives, and they then give various reasons (e.g. more effective defence, expanding the economy, protection of the environment, and so on) for the policy they prefer. We have the notorious example of the severe punishments laid upon Chinese parents who dare to have more than one child. Others argue for the need for at least replacement fertility to maintain the intergenerational tax-transfer system in order to ensure that there will be enough potential workers born to pay the taxes for the social-welfare needs of the elderly. So parents should be encouraged to have just enough children to ensure a supply of future taxpayers. As well, some argue that the nation will eventually disappear if insufficient children are born to replace those who die; to which one response might be to rely more on immigration.

The danger we see in all such arguments is that they depend, ultimately, upon political assumptions or ideologies that entail putting the family and its fertility at the service of political ends. Those ends are taken to be superior to the fertility decisions that might otherwise be made by individual couples in the absence of government-manipulated rewards or punishments. There is a heavy burden of proof of overwhelming public benefit laid upon governments that seek to re-order the procreational choices of private couples in order to enforce a preferred political vision. In addition to this, there is the notorious 'natural' variability of fertility across generations for reasons that are not fully understood, so that population targets and policies are likely to be upset by all sorts of unforeseen consequences and unanticipated exogenous variables.

A successful argument for public support of families with children must therefore be grounded in justice and equity rather than public utility, ideology or political fashions. In those terms, the question is whether families with dependent children have a claim in justice to special treatment, to some measure of public relief or support; a claim brought to prominence by the great changes of the last century.

The Child as Citizen and Taxpayer

The argument from justice or entitlement for public relief from part of the costs of child-rearing hinges upon the **citizenship** status of the child, and the **agency** or guardianship status of the parents. If a child born in this country to parents who have Australian citizenship is to be regarded as a true, if immature and legally minor, citizen of the country, then he must acquire the rights and duties of an Australian citizen. Accordingly, among his entitlements and responsibilities, but held in trust for him and exercised on his behalf by his parents as agents for him, are those of the **taxpayer**. Included in the latter status is the obligation not only to pay tax on income above a certain threshold received in his name, but also the right to an exemption from taxation below the income-tax threshold (presently $5400 annually); an income threshold traditionally regarded as the point below which all income is needed simply to survive, so that taxation on income below the threshold would threaten survival.

So children have a place in the tax system, but their immaturity requires that their parents or guardians assume that place as their legal agents, surrogates or trustees and, in that capacity, accrue to themselves both the obligations and entitlements, including the taxation treatment, due in principle to their children. If the child's 'income' consists entirely of the food, clothing, shelter and various forms of care it receives from its parents, and if the money equivalent of that income would not exceed the tax threshold, that income should, in principle, be tax-exempt. But that 'exemption', on the basis of the argument above, should accrue to the parents and, accordingly, that portion of the parents' income 'transferred' to the child should be free of tax, quite independently of, and additional to, the threshold exemptions available to the parents on their own behalf.

The foregoing is an argument justifying in principle a parental claim to tax-exemption rights exercised on behalf of the children for whom they are agents and trustees. It is also a 'horizontal equity' argument. Many taxation systems, including our own, have long granted various rebates and allowances to parents in respect of their children, but the reasoning behind the measures has usually remained obscure and ad hoc. Actual policies in Australia have become increasingly grudging and incoherent. It is important, therefore, that the justifications for such measures be carefully and explicitly spelt out. Given, then, that the principle is just and equitable, its practical and sensible implementation ought to recognise two modifying factors: first, that children do not have adult needs and responsibilities; and second, that the actual 'survival' costs of children within an already-established household are not comparable with those of adults. Consequently, the taxation and welfare treatment of families with dependent children should acknowledge these differences by entitlement to a tax-exemption threshold (or some comparable form of treatment) on behalf of their children that is **less** than that for adults.

Two further issues arise. First, having established what should be an appropriate child tax threshold (a question taken up later), should it be the same for all children? That is, should rich parents be entitled to the same dependent-child threshold as poor parents? We would argue, again on grounds of equity as between 'child taxpayers', that they should, **provided the income-tax system remains progressive** in all other respects.

The second question that arises with all changes to taxation systems concerns the effect on revenues, and incidence. If revenues are to remain the same, then obviously there must be changes in the incidence of taxation elsewhere in the system. We believe that there is scope for changes elsewhere in the revenue-expenditure systems that would deliver child-threshhold justice, improve overall taxation and distributive equity, and maintain virtual revenue neutrality. How this might be achieved is discussed later.

The Social Value of Effectively-Reared Children

If we believe that the decision to have children should be wholly private and entirely at the discretion of the parents, without manipulation of incentives or disincentives in the matter by governments, then we may assume that having children will reflect the parents' belief that such children are a 'private good' for the benefit of the parents and possibly other family members. It is nevertheless the case that children create 'externalities', as the economists put it; that is to say, they inevitably have effects outside their own families, as they grow up and enter schools, work and society in general, that may be generally beneficial or otherwise. It is therefore not a matter of indifference to us what kinds of citizens they become. The more extensive their skills and knowledge, the better their socialisation, the more law-abiding they are, the greater will be their contribution to the social and economic well-being of the nation; social life for all will be more congenial than it might otherwise be and the 'human capital' of the country will be larger, with greater potential for contributing to total national wealth.

The next step is to ask what constitutes an effectively reared child in this sense. Let us assume that there would be little argument that such a child would have the following characteristics and capacities. He/she would be:

- emotionally stable and secure with normal capacities for affection and for confident, trusting and cooperative human relationships;

- physically healthy;
- aware of, and generally conforming to, social, cultural and moral norms appropriate to his/her age;
- in age-average command of the national language and educable; and
- prepared and ready to benefit from formal education.

All that we know of child development indicates overwhelmingly that a child's acquisition of these characteristics requires intense inputs of adult labour, time, money, skill, dedication, affection and concern for the welfare of the child.

In principle, such adult services, essential for effective rearing, could be bought in the market or supplied by government. But, in fact, it seems that supply from market or government sources in the quantities and with the qualities required entails considerable difficulties and high costs. As the evidence quoted earlier suggests, the stubborn, simple, biological and social facts are that mothers and fathers (or close relatives) have been shown over and over again to be those best equipped and motivated to combine intense labour, self-sacrifice and love in advancing the development of those characteristics and capacities that define the effectively reared child. This is not to say that strangers are incapable of providing a level of care, even for long and sustained periods, but only that this is, as a generalised substitute for parental care, less than optimal as a child-rearing regime and very costly. As Becker and Murphy (1988:3) put it:

> Parental altruism is the reason why essentially all societies have shown more common sense than Plato and given parents or other close relatives primary responsibility for child care. Altruistic parents are good caretakers because they consider the effects of their actions on the welfare of children. They sometimes sacrifice their own consumption and comfort to increase that of their children.

To summarise:

- The production and rearing of children has important social consequences.
- The desirable social consequences of children and the human capital of the nation are maximised if children are reared effectively.

- The natural parents or close relatives have been shown to be those best equipped to make decisions and take actions to rear children effectively, especially babies.

- Social, political and economic changes have raised the costs of children and reduced their private benefits to parents.

- There is a case in justice for recognising children as taxpayers, for treating their parents as surrogates for their children's tax-threshold entitlements and therefore for granting tax concessions for child-rearing costs to the parents.

The Principles of Public Support for Parental Child-Rearing

The desirable social effects of children are promoted by effectively reared children. Close parental care and the economic circumstances of parents are crucial factors determining these effects. At least part of the costs of child rearing to parents is a legitimate claim against the public purse. There is thus a strong case for policies that acknowledge this by giving appropriate public support for parenting costs unless doing so would create incentives for actions that are, in other respects, socially or economically counterproductive. This possibility will be explored later.

I have offered the view that families are voluntary associations whose liberty and well-being depend upon a high degree of autonomy. Their autonomy is a condition of their capacity to become centres of fulfilment for their members and depends upon their being able to acquire and dispose their own resources fairly and with a minimum of interference.

Children are both 'private goods' and immature citizens. They are entitled to just treatment, and the parents' role as trustee and surrogate for the child's citizenship rights places power over the child in the parents' hands and places considerable obligations upon them. The ways in which children are reared has implications for the protection of their rights and for the character of the society in which they live. This is revealed, for example, in the way society protects the child's right to education. So the decision to have children cannot be taken casually and should entail, for their parents, various moral obligations, and some economic calculations and economic costs that cannot be wholly transferred to the public purse. But, equally, the having of children — the creation of immature 'citizen-taxpayers' with their own claims to civil rights — should not be a prospect so disproportionately burdensome as to tip the scales in the direction of determinedly punishing parenthood and families. This would clearly be oppressive and unfair. A policy that seeks to find the right balance would need to have the following features:

- in conformity with the principle of family autonomy, it should not offer incentives that work against family integrity, or against flexibility and choice in intra-family decision-making;

- it should hold all parents jointly responsible for the care of their dependent children; and

- the taxation of family income should allow credit for a significant proportion of the additional costs borne by parents in effectively rearing their children (or, as we might also put it, acting as agents and trustees for immature citizens and taxpayers with rights that they are too young and resourceless to defend).

The Tax Bias Against Two-Parent Families

The strong case, based on public interest and fairness, for collective support for parental child-rearing costs is very inadequately recognised by existing public policy, which, in most respects, contravenes the three guiding principles proposed above.

A number of studies (Castles, 1987; Jordan, 1987; Bradbury et al., 1989; Tapper, 1990b) have shown conclusively that existing taxation and welfare policies, rather than giving equitable aid to two-parent families with dependent children, actively discriminate against them by working to reduce their 'equivalent incomes' in comparison with the childless, those whose children have grown up, and the aged. For example, in 1991 it was estimated that the aged population eligible (subject to means testing) for service or aged persons pensions comprised 1 463 106 females aged 60 or above and 811 183 males aged 65 or above (ignoring those former veterans aged 60 or more who, subject to means testing, were eligible for service pensions). This group, totalling 2 274 289 persons, were allocated pensions totalling $12.7 billion — or $5586 per person. The actual figure per person would be higher when those not eligible after means testing were removed from the group. The comparable figure for family allowances and supplements (excluding sole parent pensions and allowances) was approximately $2 billion for about four million children under 16, or about $500 per child (ABS, 1991b; Budget Statements, 1991–92).

Tapper (1990b, 1991), using Jordan's (1987) evidence, shows that, after balancing taxation paid against public benefits received, the real living standards of average parents and their dependent children have been reduced to about three fifths of the living standards of the rest of the adult working population. This is summarised in Figure 6. Even if we allow, as suggested earlier, that parents should not be **wholly** compensated for the costs of child rearing, this nevertheless appears grossly unbalanced and contrary to the rule of tax fairness that equal living standards should be equally taxed.

The plain fact is that in intact families with dependent children and one wage earner, a single income has to support three or more persons, yet the significance of this for median incomes is barely and inadequately recognised by the taxation and welfare systems.

But, paradoxically and inequitably enough, as Tapper (1990b) has observed, when families separate, relatively lavish government aid is provided for the children of separated parents from welfare funds derived largely from taxation levied upon intact families with dependent children. Census figures for 1986 (ABS, 1989a) show that there were 3 043 600 dependent children in intact families and 403 000 in sole-parent families (a ratio of 7.5:1). The 1991–92 federal budget provides $1.965 billion in allowances for children in intact families and $2.924 billion for sole-parent pensions and allowances (Budget Statements, 1991). So if dependent children in intact families received support on the same scale as those in sole-parent families, the government would have to find an extra $20 billion. To put it another way, the federal government gives about ten times as much support to children of parents who have separated as to those of parents who stay together. And it will be remembered that there is no evidence that divorced or separated parents, as a class of couples, are poorer than parents who stay together. Although a spouse claiming a pension is required to 'take reasonable steps' to secure maintenance support from the absent partner, this is often not forthcoming because the partner/ former-or-separated spouse cannot be traced, is unemployed, or refuses to meet his or her obligations. The Child Support Scheme, intended to deal with these issues, has had only partial success in meeting this problem. The upshot is that the pension and allowances may be paid to parents who, jointly considered, are no less financially able to care for their children than parents who stay together.

In this way, current family policy not only denies equity, it handicaps the capacity of parents of intact families effectively to raise their children; it diminishes the creation of the human capital on which the future of the nation depends; and, by promising government support for separated parents, it provides an unintended incentive for family break-up.

Figure 6
Benefits and taxes per household

For selected household types (average, $ per week)
Bar width is proportional to the number of households in each category

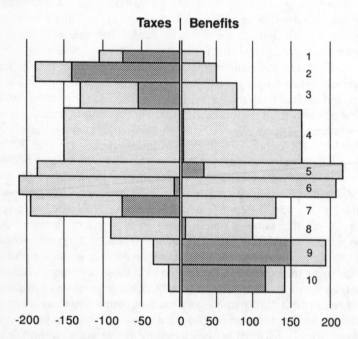

Composition of the selected Household Types:

1 Young single (one person living alone, age under 35).

2 Young married couple (no children, household head aged under 35).

3 Couple and child(ren) under 5 years.

4 Couple and child(ren), eldest aged between 5 and 15).

5 Couple and dependent child(ren), eldest aged 15 or more.

6 Couple and both dependent and non-dependent children
   (but no other household members).

7 Couple and non-dependent child(ren).

8 Middle-aged couple (head aged between 55 and 64).

9 Elderly couple (head aged 65 or more).

10 Elderly single (one person living alone, aged 65 or more).

Source: Tapper, 1990a:113

Chapter 11

Out-Of-Home Child Care

It was claimed earlier that there is a strong case for public allowances or concessions to parents in meeting the costs of child-rearing unless doing so would create incentives that were, in other respects, socially or economically counterproductive. Some have argued, in effect, (Anstie, et al., 1988) that subsidies directed towards parents are counterproductive in this way if they induce one parent (more usually, mothers) to stay out of the workforce or to leave it because the subsidies reduce the opportunity costs of not working and society therefore loses the economic value of their workforce production. But this ignores the fact that, although people who work contribute to production, they also remove a roughly corresponding amount in the form of market consumption.

There is, however, a separate question about the value of home production as compared to the value of commercial or industrial production. It is difficult to see how such comparisons and calculations could be conclusively made. No doubt a nominal or putative figure can be established by allocating an arbitrary wages-per-hour value to housework and child care to yield some kind of rough comparison. This the Australian Bureau of Statistics (1990) has done, and it came up with a figure estimating the value of housework in 1986–87 at somewhere between $137 billion and $163 billion, more than half as much again as **officially** measured Gross Domestic Product. An international analysis by the OECD (1992), valuing household time at the (low) rate of a maid, estimates that the value of household work would add between one third and one half to the Gross Domestic Product of the five large countries studied, a figure consistent with the Australian findings. One is dealing here with home-produced goods and services that are not even taken into account in the conventional economics of Gross Domestic Product or Gross National Income. This has some bizarre consequences. As *The Economist* notes (1992): 'if a man marries his cleaner, turning a paid employee into an unpaid housewife, then GDP falls instantly even though much the same work gets done'.

Following this line of thought, how much of the measured growth of GDP in the 1980s, for example, was the consequence of family breakdown or taxation-induced economic stress that drives wives and mothers into the workforce where their wages are counted as an addition to GDP or GNI, but the loss of home amenity or more effective child care is not counted as a subtraction? Wages are counted, but work that brings no salary is treated as economically irrelevant. Often, then, an increase in human distress, or reduced human-capital formation, might come to be measured as a contribution to national 'growth'! Perversely enough, marriage and/or parenthood may thus entail a reduction in **measured** GDP if the spouse or parent leaves the salaried workforce, no matter what goods and services, no matter how much more welfare, he or she produces in the (officially unmeasured) home economy.

There is a very real sense in which to embark upon a putative valuation of what is done in the home is to give undue importance to a utilitarian calculus. Is love and care of children, husbands and wives, part of a service industry? Is it more or less valuable than a hamburger or radio? However we make these judgments, there is absolutely no convincing argument that workforce production is more valuable, in terms of overall human welfare, than home production and child care. A judicious balance between them would seem to maximise human and family welfare; and where the balance should be set for any particular family is a matter that only that family can decide, as free as possible of officially-contrived incentives to tip the balance one way or the other. Consequently, there is no case for favouring out-of-home child-care subsidies in order to make it easier for women to join the workforce, as against a universal subsidy to all parents, whether working or not, to spend as they see fit on child and family welfare.

Child-Rearing Subsidies and Freedom of Choice

That being so, and accepting the principle of parental entitlement to such a subsidy (whether directly or in the form of a tax concession), I would argue that policy should seek to be neutral in all respects about how that subsidy is used within families; whether one family uses it, say, for clothing while another family buys child care so that the mother can work part-time or full-time. This would be consistent with the principle of family autonomy and the absence of official incentives that might prejudice flexibility and choice in intra-family decision-making.

But, in fact, public policy is not neutral in these matters. First, as we have shown, the unfair tax treatment of intact families directly reduces their relative standard of living and therefore provides a strong incentive for both parents to join the workforce. Second, the policies of the federal government in relation to publicly-funded child care **are explicitly based on supporting labour-market participation by mothers** (Commonwealth Department of Health, Housing and Community Services, 1992:5). To this end, the federal government has budgeted child-care expenditures totalling $375 million for 1991–92, rising to $488 million for 1994–95 (Budget Statements, 1991:103–9). Although our focus here is on federal government policy, child-care expenditure by some States is very significant. New South Wales, for example, gave assistance in the order of $142 million for formal child care in 1989–90, an average outlay of about $1060 for each of some 134 000 children receiving subsidised care (Hogbin Ercole et al., 1991:10).

In moving towards child-care subsidies conditional upon mothers joining the industrial workforce, the federal government is unfairly discriminating against mothers not in the labour force (either because they cannot find work or do not seek it); and, here too, the subsidies will be derived in significant part from the taxes of single-income families with dependent children. This apparent inequity is offset to some extent by the dependent spouse and dependent child maximum rebate of $1412 annually, which cuts out at a level of spousal income of $5929 annually and which, as we shall see, is overshadowed in generosity by the child-care aid available to some, and not, at the moment, confined to working mothers. For a strange feature of the present system is that formal, out-of-home child care is used predominantly by families in which only one parent is in employment (ABS, 1987). In other words, its function in these circumstances, whether intended or not, is to provide child-free leisure for a non-working spouse. Presumably this will contract as government policy seeks to favour working mothers.

But the main point is the very substantial subsidies concentrated upon that relatively small proportion of parents seeking, and fortunate enough to have access to, child-care centres and public subsidies for operating costs and fee relief. Jones (1988:5) puts the average recurrent cost to the Commonwealth of a child-care place in 1987–88 at $1908 per child, while Teal (1990:22) has calculated that 'Every child in a public child care centre received a subsidy of some $0.66/hour while the average subsidy for those on fee relief was $2.28/hour. Thus for the children on average fee relief the subsidy paid was about $2500/child/year and for those not on fee relief it was about $770/child/year'. For a family earning less than $399 a week and with one child in long-day care, the federal government provides $4420 annually in fee relief (Budget Statements, 1991:3–108. Senator Peter Walsh has claimed (1992) that 'The actual cost, including a capital allowance, of caring for under-two-year-olds in a long day care centre is almost $200 a week. This cost is hidden from consumers by cross-subsidy'.

The bias against families that choose not to use out-of-home child care is again evident in the fact that family allowance for a family of four children cuts out at a family income of $68 000 annually while child-care subsidies for families with fewer children are still payable at family incomes in excess of $70 000 annually.

Once again we confront the incoherence of family policy. One incentive (dependent-spouse rebate) works to keep one parent at home while another incentive — the very substantial child-care subsidies taken up and used by **some** working mothers and, at least for the time being, **some** non-working mothers — helps some to work and some to enjoy their leisure more fully, with no apparent consideration for the contradictions and inequities involved. At the same time, subsidies are available for out-of-home child care for relatively well-off families but not for in-home care by families who are less well off.

Employer-Provided Child Care

Budgetary constraints, and the mounting cost of government child-care subsidies **selectively delivered to some classes of beneficiaries**, is leading politicians and special-interest groups to look to industry to pick up some of the costs and to provide extra facilities, in cooperation with federal, State and local governments.

The federal government is currently providing income-tested fee relief to parents using employer-sponsored child-care services. For this purpose it has budgeted just on $59 million for 1991–92 to cover both employer-sponsored and commercial services. The New South Wales and Victorian governments are providing $1.5 million and $1.8 million respectively for the development of private-sector and public-sector employer-sponsored pilot projects.

In 1991, the National Women's Consultative Council issued a paper (1991) prepared for it by Community Child Care, Victoria, which recommended that initiatives of this sort be extended, with federal support, to include joint child-care ventures by employers and local-government authorities. The same paper further recommended that the federal government consider introducing an Industry Child Care Levy to fund places reserved for employers to allocate to their employees in community child-care centres.

In addition to fee relief, the federal government gives a variety of tax concessions to foster employer-provided child-care services. These include favourable depreciation rates on capital expenditures for employer-established child-care centres; writing-off of construction costs; exemption from fringe-benefits tax for facilities for employees' children provided on the employers' premises and also for payments for priority access to child-care places for employees; deductions of payments made to community or commercial centres contracted to provide for employees' children; and deduction of management fees for centres provided by an employer.

Confused Objectives, Inefficiencies and Restriction of Choice

The intentions and rationale of this policy are perplexing. If it is in an employer's interests to pay the costs of child care in order to attract or retain personnel, he will do it without subsidies and the provision of the subsidy is therefore wasteful. If meeting the costs himself suits his interests, his next question is: 'What **form** should this take?' And it is clear that, except perhaps for very large employers, the most efficient course would be to pay all or part of the costs of purchasing child-care services from a specialist supplier suitable to the employee, rather than go into the business of setting up a child-care service himself, a field in which he has no expertise.

If it is not in the interests of an employer to pay child-care costs for an employee, what interest is being served by the elaborate and administratively costly tax-concession and subsidy arrangements that could not be more flexibly and efficiently served by the government subsidising the employee, **directly**, to purchase the child care that suited him or her? Apart from the delusion that expenses transferred to 'business' are not ultimately borne by individuals, one suspects that, in targeting concessions and subsidies to employers, the objectives of government might be, first, to incrementally impose child-care costs on employers through regulation while sweetening the pill with some concessions, and second, to further shape the choices of women with dependent children towards workforce participation.

The overall picture, then, is of very substantial subsidies and tax expenditures targeted towards facilitating employer-provided child care and the encouragement of mothers into the workforce: in other words, of policies that, even if they do not entail any **direct** increase in total taxation, depend upon redirecting tax revenue from **all** taxpayers to fund highly specific objectives chosen, not by the principals (parents and corporations), but by those bureaucracies and interest groups that have gained control of the tax dollars and the regulatory agenda. For individuals, corporations and families, options are being ruled out as the balance of incentives is tipped further against variable and freely-negotiated contracts between employer and employee, and against the choice of home care of children and home production of goods, in favour of out-of-home care, the two-income family and workforce production of goods.

The Wider Implications

The National Women's Consultative Council's canvassing of an 'Industry Child Care Levy' is a significant straw in the wind about the directions that government might take. We have the examples of other levies — the Training Guarantee Levy and the Superannuation Guarantee Levy, for instance — that impose costs and inefficiencies on business, constrain managerial decision-making and disposal of resources, and ultimately redirect income out of the hands of ordinary taxpayers, workers and parents towards politically chosen expenditures and particular occupational groups and interests — in this case, child-care professionals, bureaucrats and others who stand to benefit from regulation and 'credentialism' within the child-care industry. This is, of course, part of a more general trend that is destroying choice and flexibility and is, in effect, increasing the burden of 'taxation' without formally imposing a tax as such.

The purpose of conventional, direct government taxation is to acquire a portion of private income and to redirect expenditure of the money to ends chosen by government. But if the government eliminates the step of actually getting the money into its own hands and, instead, orders the taxpayer, whether a private individual or a corporation, to use his or its money for some specific purpose imposed by government regulations, then it is 'taxing' just as effectively as if it took the money first; but the funds so controlled do not show up as government revenue. Ultimately, the whole burden of inefficiencies and extra costs falls not upon the abstraction called 'the corporation', but upon individuals, those who consume the corporation's products and those workers who miss out on wage increases, or who surrender some control of their incomes, or who lose their jobs if the corporation fails or if the value of their labour falls below the cost of employing them.

An 'industry child-care levy' would take its place among those anti-employment and dependency-inducing policies, such as minimum wages, restrictive practices and tariffs, that are damaging family autonomy and the effective formation of human capital. The notion also highlights the confusion of governments that wring their hands about the 'need for exports' as they cripple industries with avoidable regulatory costs and employee on-costs that make them internationally uncompetitive.

Credentialism and Child Care

A major threat to affordability, choice and flexibility in child-care arrangements is emerging from the interest-group push for 'quality' child care and the placing of stringent 'accreditation' requirements on child-care providers, both community-based and private. The federal government has moved rapidly to establish an Accreditation System for Long-Day-Care centres and its Interim National Accreditation Council has produced documents setting out possible guidelines and criteria for measuring and monitoring facilities and services of child-care centres and the qualifications of service-providers.

If past experience is any guide, these moves are the typical portents of a federal regulatory push into yet another area of enterprise that has so far managed satisfactorily without it. It also foreshadows the elbowing-out of parental criteria of what constitutes satisfactory child care and the substitution of bureaucratic and interest-group-influenced criteria that serve those interests. It represents a further attack on the presumption that parents in general are those most competent and assiduous in judging and determining what is best for their children and their own interests in the choosing of child care-arrangements. In any case, long-day-care centres are already regulated by State governments and there is no evidence that further federal regulation would serve any useful purpose. Even if it did, it is quite possible that the costs would outweigh any marginal benefits.

Finally, accreditation, especially if made compulsory, would certainly raise the costs of child care if it lifts the formal qualifications (and hence the training costs and salary expectations) of child-care providers, and if it mandates more elaborate buildings (especially if suitable only for child care), more space per child, more equipment and enlarged service requirements. These raised costs would be paid for by parents directly if they are not in receipt of a government fee subsidy. But if the whole or part of the raised costs is offset by an increase in the fee subsidy to qualifying parents, this increased subsidy would necessarily be paid for by all taxpayers, including parents who do not or cannot take advantage of out-of-home child care of the kind in question. This would simply aggravate the present inequity (and iniquity) referred to earlier.

Any federal insistence on care-provider qualifications in excess of those satisfying parental customers would represent an additional cost without any corresponding benefits and a further unnecessary impost upon parents and taxpayers. The excessively credentialled care provider would reap an unjustified income increase at the expense of taxpayers and parents.

Child Care and Parental Autonomy

If we refuse to follow Plato's advice to put children under the care of the state and its agents from birth, and if we agree, with occasional special exceptions, that their natural parents are far and away the best people to look after them, it seems to follow that parents should have maximum autonomy to make the rearing and child-care decisions that seem best to them, given their individual family circumstances and preferences.

There are no good reasons, economic, social or equitable, why public policy should seek to shape that decision-making towards encouraging both parents into the workforce if that is not what they wish. On the contrary, there are arguments against such a course. But be that as it may, in the interests of preserving neutrality for parental decision-making, there is, equally, no good reason why one or other parent should be persuaded to stay home by official inducements (the dependent-spouse rebate, for instance) if that is contrary to what they would otherwise see as the best course of action.

Some might argue that women are liberated by being induced into the workforce and away from home care of children and home production. But if liberation is made concrete in free choice, without influence by officially contrived incentives to act one way rather than another, then creating the circumstance where such choices can be individually made in terms of individual preferences is the way to go. This means, so far as women are concerned, that the state should place neither inducements nor impediments before a woman deciding about either course of action in accordance with her preferences.

Yet our discussion above shows a powerful array of official inducements for mothers to go into the workforce, against a relatively weak array of inducements (primarily the dependent-spouse rebate) to stay home. In my view, both are wrong insofar as they seek to shape choice one way or the other, and it is a compounding of this wrong for government to weight the incentives deliberately and explicitly in one direction. Despite this, mothers of young children loudly declare their preferences by resisting these inducements to a surprising degree. About 68 per cent of childless wives in their twenties are in the workforce. When such women have children, this drops to 36 per cent after the first child and to just 4 per cent after the second child (Evans, 1988:4).

What, then, is to be done?

I would argue that policy should recognise and act upon my central contentions. The first of these is that there is a collective responsibility to acknowledge the child's just claim (as citizen) to equitable treatment, which means, in practice, helping parents rear their dependent children effectively. The second is that the natural parents are primarily and jointly responsible for the care of their dependent children, and that their decisions, within the law, about how they should meet their responsibilities should not be shaped by official inducements to act one way rather than another.

In other words, all parents of dependent children should be treated equally; all should be entitled to the same level of subsidy or tax concessions in respect of each child; and no group's treatment or concessions should be made conditional upon making career or family choices favoured by the state.

Chapter 12

Forms of Support, Taxation and Equity

The time has come to take up the further questions, foreshadowed above, concerning the level of tax-threshold treatment of children's 'income' from their parents and therefore of the tax and benefits positions of parents with dependent children. Such questions also involve the revenue effects of changing the present system, the position of rich and poor parents, and related matters.

Public acknowledgement of a collective responsibility for parental child rearing has been put into practice in a variety of ways — by the 'family wage' or 'basic wage' of earlier times, by child endowment, child allowances, rebates for dependent spouses and children, sole-parent pensions, family-allowance supplements, and, more recently, relatively lavish child-care subsidies (the last of these delivered haphazardly and selectively in a variety of forms for various ends, with both intended and unintended consequences). It all adds up to a history of policies that are frequently changing, inconsistent, complicated, expensive to administer and demonstrably inequitable. Reform, with simplification and the straightforward delivery of equity, is long overdue.

Whatever form a reformed method of support might take, it should be based on the presumption that parenting, whether within the married state or outside it, is a joint enterprise from whose responsibilities neither parent can unilaterally opt out without penalty. Public policy should provide support for parenting and rearing children as the parents see fit, within the law. Given these as operating principles, the support should be the **only** form of collective assistance in meeting child rearing and child-care costs.

Rationalising Child-Rearing Support and Abolishing the Dependent-Spouse Rebate

It follows that all other government subsidies and tax concessions for out-of-home child care should be abolished and replaced by this single, universal form of child-rearing assistance, on the understanding, of course, that the parents may use it towards purchasing out-of-home child care if they wish or for any other purpose — education, general family purposes, or whatever.

Consistently with this approach, dependent-spouse rebates should also be abolished. There is no good reason why those without dependent children should be encouraged to stay home or that home production should be advantaged over market production, in the absence of children. But what kind of support should be given to replace all others?

The Child Tax Credit/Benefit

Of the various forms, the one that best meets the requirements for simplicity, universality, equity and avoidance of poverty traps is the 'child tax credit'. For low-income families, the child tax credit, in the form to be described below, efficiently and simply serves the purposes of other welfare payments, such as family allowances and family-allowance supplements, without creating poverty traps and disincentives to seeking employment. Within a progressive tax system, the rich would continue to be taxed more heavily; yet the child tax credit would be equitable in that it treats all children, of the rich and poor alike, as equally valuable and deserving of the same consideration from the tax and welfare systems.

Under a tax-credit system, those earning incomes that are high enough to be taxable can deduct the amount of the tax credit from the tax that would otherwise be payable. So, if the child tax credit is set, say, at $2000 annually per dependent child, and if a single-income family has a tax bill of $7000 and one dependent child, the payable tax bill is reduced to $5000. If an otherwise comparable family has an income too low to incur taxation, it of course pays no tax and receives a cash payment of $2000; while a family in an intermediate position would be treated pro rata, paying reduced taxation **and** receiving some cash-in-hand, the total benefit being equivalent, as with the other examples, to $2000.

The appropriate terminology is problematic here since the 'child tax credit' is really a mixture of benefit (for the poor) and tax credit for those required to pay tax. So we will refer to it as the 'tax credit/benefit'. But the key point is that it is intended to be an equitable and universal way of providing child-rearing support predicated on joint parenting, irrespective of the marital status of the parents.

Sole Parents and the Tax Credit/Benefit

Accordingly, the position of sole or supporting parents needs some consideration. They would, of course, receive the tax/credit benefit in common with all other parents with dependent children. It would clearly be inequitable, therefore, that they should receive an extra, exclusive benefit in the form of Supporting Parents Benefit — a benefit paid for in large part from the incomes of two-parent families — simply because the other parent has sought to escape his or her parenting responsibilities. We have seen that the Child Support Scheme has helped but still falls short of dealing with the situation. Many who qualify for support do not register to seek it and, of those who do, many do not receive the sums they are entitled to. Accordingly, the taxpayer meets the shortfall. Payment of the proposed child tax credit/benefit to the custodial parent could perhaps be made dependent upon the other parent being identified, 'registered' and fully incorporated into the Child Support Scheme.

If, despite the best efforts of all concerned, it is impossible to secure maintenance from the absent parent, special additional public support for sole parents can be justified only if the sole parent is unable to enter the workforce full- or part-time because one or other of his or her children is in infancy and it is against the child's interest that it should be separated from the parent for more than a few hours. The extra assistance in such cases, equivalent to single person's unemployment benefit, should cease when the child is old enough to go to school.

Once again, the intention is to treat all children equally in terms of the support they get from the state and not to advantage one form of family life at the expense of another or to create incentives that encourage unnecessary dependency or lead to behaviours that work against the welfare of children and the integrity and autonomy of families.

Tax Equity and Family Welfare

The foregoing discussion has sought to clarify the principles underlying the case for public support for child-rearing and child-care costs and the way in which that support might most equitably and efficiently be delivered. I have argued that equity and efficiency are to be interpreted in a 'practical' sense on the supposition that the autonomous nuclear family is the best judge and deliverer of its own and its children's welfare. In so judging and acting it is the most appropriate agent for the creation of the nation's human capital. The argument from justice justifies public support in meeting part of the child-rearing costs of parents.

But for many years economic policy, welfare policy and taxation policy have dealt very badly with the average family's economic welfare, its autonomy and its ability to make free and authentic judgments in its own best interests. Policy, especially in relation to child-rearing costs and child care, has been inconsistent, unfair and strongly biased towards driving both parents into the workforce and towards choosing child care options that are expensive, restrictive on the choices of parents and enterprises, and selectively delivered in ways that are neither equitable nor socially or economically justified. The structure of incentives contrived by government seems to constitute a virtual policy of industrial recruitment (if not quite conscription), particularly for mothers whose inclination is to stay at home with their children, at least for their early years.

Implementing the Dependent Child Tax Credit/Benefit

It is time to make a fresh start by:

- treating all children equally;

- delivering the same value of child-rearing and child-care support to all parents, without specifying forms of expenditure, while avoiding poverty-trap incentives and inequities; and

- abolishing all child-care and child-rearing allowances and subsidies, including the sole-parent pension and dependent-spouse rebate, and substituting a single, new child tax-credit/benefit, fixed at $2000 per child annually, along the lines referred to above.

Why $2000? This is, to some extent, an arbitrary figure but a modest one. The actual annual cost to parents of properly raising a child from birth to school leaving age (16) is substantially more than $2000. But we have argued that children are both 'private goods' and 'taxpayers' and 'citizens' in their own right. As 'private goods' of choice, children should represent a real cost of some sort to their parents; the decision to have children should be a deliberate and responsible one and parents should therefore be not fully compensated from the public purse for the cost. But the decision to have children should not be punished; nor should the instant citizenship of the child be ignored and his/her right to adequate maintenance (or 'income') and 'taxpayer' status count for nothing. So a pragmatic balance needs to be struck and rough justice dispensed. The figure of $2000 per child annually is my judgment of an appropriate one under present economic circumstances. Obviously, it is offered here merely as a basis for discussion.

At June 30 1990, it was estimated (ABS, 1991b) that there were just on four million children aged 0–15 in Australia. An annual dependent-child tax credit/benefit of $2000 per child for this group would therefore cost about $8 billion annually. For 1992–93, the federal government has budgeted $7.725 billion for assistance to families with children (Budget Statements, 1992:3.82). This includes family allowances, family-allowance supplements, sole-parent pensions and allowances, child care, and other child payments. If, as recommended here, all of those payments were abolished with the introduction of a dependent child tax-credit/ benefit, the resulting extra cost of the scheme would be about $300 million. But this sum would be further reduced by deducting the savings from the abolition, at the same time, of the dependent-spouse and sole-parent rebates amounting to $991 million (Commonwealth Department of the Treasury, 1991). Also saved would be the cost to revenue of the various tax concessions, write-offs, and so on, allowed to employers providing child-care services for their employees. Additional significant savings would probably arise from the simplified administration of the scheme and its substantial transfer from the welfare budget to the taxation budget. The upshot would be a fair, reformed and simplified scheme that is likely to be publicly welcomed and that would deliver **savings** of government expenditure of the order of several hundred million dollars annually. In addition, in overcoming some of the poverty traps associated with family allowances and supplements, and the negative incentives of the sole-parent pension and allowances, the scheme would have positive incentive effects leading to savings and extra tax revenue from greater workforce participation.

The suggested figure of $2000 is low when considered in relation to the actual extra costs of rearing children. For the September 1990 quarter, the Institute of Family Studies (*The Sydney Morning Herald*, 28 August 1991) estimated the weekly costs of a child between the ages 0–13 as ranging from $138 to $200, depending upon the age group of the child. These figures show a large discrepancy between the value of the proposed tax credit/benefit and the estimated real costs of a child; but, nevertheless, this is at least partially acceptable under our principle that the public purse should not be obliged to meet all the costs of child-rearing.

The figure of $2000 is also low when considered as a small step towards restoring the battered condition of families whose relative tax position has deteriorated markedly over recent years. In 1954–55 a single, no-dependants taxpayer on average weekly earnings paid 9.60 per cent of his income in income tax. A man with a wife and two dependent children to support on the same average weekly wage and receiving child endowment paid virtually **no** tax (0.57 per cent). By 1985 the comparable figures had risen to 25.59 per cent and 16.97 per cent (Tapper, 1990b:44). So our figure is less than generous, but it has two great virtues: it is more equitable than the present taxation and allowance arrangements and it would save a great deal of money.

Income-Splitting for Parents?

The case for more generous treatment than we have suggested for families with dependent children is a strong one and a $2000 tax credit/benefit alone, while fairer than the existing system, would not remove present inequities. One option is to increase it. But another one is to combine the tax credit/benefit with the option of income-splitting for income-tax purposes **for married couples with pre-school dependent children only**. This would involve adopting some features of the American tax system and has some desirable incentive features.

The essence of the scheme is to have separate tax scales for individuals and families. A couple with one or more pre-school dependent children could choose to be taxed individually in the ordinary way or it could choose to file a joint return. A joint return would have a tax-free threshold of $10 800 (i.e. twice the individual thresholds of $5400) and, of course, the couple would also receive a tax credit/benefit of $2000 per child.

Towards Sound Family Policy

This combination has the virtues of:

- delivering a **cash** benefit of $2000 per annum per child to poor families, together with a large tax-free threshold, while retaining strong incentives for parents to enter or remain in the workforce, thus avoiding poverty traps;

- reducing the burden of income taxation for average families with, say, two or three young children, with obvious incentive effects, especially for single-income families;

- not disproportionately advantaging rich families over poor or average families because they would still pay more tax in proportion to their higher incomes;

- reducing the present unfairness whereby the living standards of families are taxed more highly than the living standards of singles;

- helping meet the special child-care needs of families with pre-school children;

- simplicity of administration, especially when combined with the elimination of other forms of family support; and

- discouraging casual or precipitate divorce and desertion because (i) since the filing of joint returns would be a taxation advantage and privilege confined to married couples with dependent children, divorce would entail its loss (though not the loss of the tax credit/ benefit for the custodial parent), and (ii) divorce would also entail the loss, for the non-custodial parent, of the former joint enjoyment of the tax credit/benefit.

The introduction of a child tax credit/benefit would be revenue positive, given the abolition of the other rebates and allowances, and it would also have various incentive and cost-saving effects. However, to add income-splitting, even of the limited kind suggested here, would probably increase the taxation of singles and the childless. But my scheme incorporates savings that would offset at least some of the extra taxation on this group that might be needed to maintain revenues. Just what the precise effects would be is a calculation beyond the scope of this work. There would be both negative and positive effects: possibly negative for those who do not have, or will never have, children, but positive for all children and parents, including poorer parents and children. But we are all children at one time and the overwhelming majority of us are parents at some time.

The introduction of a child tax credit/benefit is justified in terms of greater equity for families and the likelihood that that would work strongly, in the long run, towards producing the incalculable benefits of greatly enriched 'human capital', within more spontaneously stable, more autonomous, and more fairly-treated families.

Chapter 13

Conclusion

The basic objectives of this study are to consider realistic ways of:

- delivering justice in marriage and divorce;

- coming to grips with those economic and labour-market conditions that must be established in order to enable men, women and young people to find a place in the workforce — a place that will make dependence on welfare unnecessary and that will open up the possibility, if it is their choice, of a fulfilling married and family life;

- repealing the welfare-state encouragement to irresponsibility, idleness and dependency for those who are able-bodied;

- treating parents and their children fairly within the tax system; and

- eliminating a state-subsidised child-care system that is incoherent, inefficient and unfair, in that it unjustly bribes some mothers to work in industry, enables others to enjoy leisure, and requires the rest to help pay the cost while receiving nothing in return.

This study has examined the damaging and unfair consequences of national policies that are deeply entrenched, highly interactive and mutually reinforcing. Together they compose a system that generates distress unnecessarily, and persistently undermines marriage and family life, the formation of the nation's human capital and the development of a vigorous and internationally competitive economy. The centrepiece is a system of welfare benefits whose manifest function is to minimise human misery — misery caused in large part by other policies — but whose latent function is frequently to provide incentives for others to live off the state. The cost of the latter is borne in large part by ordinary families through a taxation system that has grown ever more punitive.

If the proposals distilled from my analysis and discussion of these matters are implemented, marriage and family life will be undertaken more confidently and with better prospects of success. Families with dependent children will be treated more fairly. With that will come enhanced individual and social well-being at greatly reduced cost. Among the beneficiaries will be children. Beyond attention to their basic physiological needs, their requirements are mainly moral, emotional and educational. If their parents stay together, that solves most of their problems, because intact families, given work and modest taxation, are more likely either to satisfy those requirements or more adequately to prepare their children for the social milieu that will.

The persistence of a democratic culture requires many forms and levels of independence from the state. And so, the deeper perspective, or common thread, which unites these recommendations is a view of what is fundamental to a free, culturally and morally robust, and economically vigorous society; i.e. that the final repositories, or 'true subjects', of these qualities lie outside the state in independent institutions, enterprises and associations pursuing their own ends under the rule of law. They are the loci within which, and through which, individuals may seek their own versions of fulfilment and well-being. Their independence is conditional upon the extent to which they are free under the law to acquire their own resources and to use what they have legitimately acquired to serve their lawful ends. If government taxes them unduly, or so hems them in with regulations and counterproductive incentives that they become flaccid and paralysed, they will languish and decay. This is as true of the voluntary association of the family as of any other. I believe that the reforms proposed here could begin to arrest and reverse the decay that is already well established. If they are implemented, all of us will be better off in the longer term.

References

Anstie, R., R. Gregory, S. Dowrick & J. Pincus (1988), 'Government Spending on Work-Related Child Care: Some Economic Issues', Centre for Economic Policy Research, Australian National University (Discussion Paper No. 191).

Australian Bureau of Statistics (ABS) (1986), *Australian Demographic Trends*, Canberra (Catalogue No.3102.0).

—— (1987), *Child Care Arrangements Australia*, Canberra (Catalogue No. 4402.0).

—— (1989a), *Census 86 — Australian Families and Households*, Canberra, (Catalogue No.2506.0).

—— (1989b), *1988 Births Australia*, Canberra (Catalogue No. 3301.0).

—— (1989c), *1988 Marriages Australia*, Canberra Catalogue No. 3306.0).

—— (1989d), *1988 Divorces Australia*, Canberra Catalogue No. 3307.0).

—— (1990), 'Measuring Unpaid Household Work: Issues and Experimental Estimates', Canberra (Information Paper No. 5236.0).

—— (1991a), *Labour Force Status and Other Characteristics of Families Australia*, Canberra (Catalogue No. 6224.0).

—— (1991b), *Estimated Resident Population by Sex and Age States and Territories of Australia June 1990 and Preliminary June 1991*, Canberra (Catalogue No. 3201.0).

—— (1992a), *Child Care, Australia November 1990*, Canberra (Catalogue No. 4402.0).

—— (1992b), *1991 Divorces Australia*, (Canberra Catalogue No. 3307.0).

—— (1992c), *Average Weekly Earning States and Australia*, Canberra (Catalogue No. 6302.0).

Barry, N. (1988), 'An Individualist's View of Marriage and the Family', *CIS Policy Report* 4(6): 37–9.

Bauer, G. (1992), *Washington Watch*, Family Research Council, 4 June.

Becker, G. & K. Murphy (1988), 'The Family and the State', *Journal of Law & Economics* 31: 1–18.

Belsky, J. (1986), *Zero to Three*, National Center for Clinical Infant Programs, Washington, D.C.

Bowlby, J. (1982), *Attachment and Loss*, Basic Books, New York.

Bradbury, B. et al. (1989), *Trends in the Disposable Incomes of Australian Families, 1982–83 to 1989–90*, Social Welfare Research Centre, University of New South Wales, Sydney.

Budget Statements 1991–92 (1991), *Budget Paper No. 1*, Commonwealth of Australia, AGPS, Canberra.

Budget Statements 1992–93 (1992), *Budget Paper No. 1*, Commonwealth of Australia, AGPS, Canberra.

Carmichael, Gordon A., (1986), 'Marriage Intentions of Young Australians', *Australian Journal of Sex, Marriage & Family*, 7 (2),71-82.

Castles, I. (1987), 'Government Welfare Outlays: Who Benefits? Who Pays?', *Canberra Bulletin of Public Administration*, May: 47–57.

Cherlin, A. et al. (1991), 'Longitudinal Studies of the Effects of Divorce on Children in Great Britain and the United States', *Science* 252: 1386–9.

Commonwealth Department of Health, Housing and Community Services (1992), 'Commonwealth child care fee relief and operational subsidies: an issues paper', February, Canberra.

Commonwealth Department of Social Security (1991), *Annual Report*, Canberra.

Commonwealth Department of the Treasury (1991), *Tax Expenditures Statement*, Canberra.

Cox, J. (1992), *Private Welfare*, Centre for Independent Studies, Sydney.

Davis, G. & M. Murch (1988), *Grounds for Divorce*, Clarendon Press, Oxford.

Denning, Lord (1980), *The Due Process of Law*, Butterworths, London.

Dennis, N. & G. Erdos (1992), *Families without Fatherhood*, The Institute of Economic Affairs Health and Welfare Unit, London.

Eastman, M. (1989), *Family: The Vital Factor*, Collins Dove, Melbourne.

Economic Planning Advisory Council (EPAC) (1992), *Unemployment in Australia*, AGPS, Canberra (Council Paper no. 51).

The Economist (1992), 'The Value of Drudgery', 4 July: 60.

Evans, M. (1988), 'Married Women in the Workforce', *National Social Science Survey Report* 1(2): 4-5 (Research School of Social Sciences, Australian National University).

——— (1989), 'Why Married Women Work', *National Social Science Survey Report* 1(3): 6-8 (Research School of Social Sciences, Australian National University).

Fagan, D. (1990), 'Discretions Should Go', *Australian Law News*, April: 12–16.

Family Law Act 1975.

Finlay, H. & R. Bailey-Harris (1989), *Family Law in Australia*, Butterworths, Sydney.

Gilder, G. (1981), *Wealth and Poverty*, Basic Books, New York.

Gill, R. (1992), 'For the sake of the children', *The Public Interest* 108 (Summer): 81–96.

Green, D. (1991), 'Liberty, Poverty and the Underclass: A Classical-Liberal Approach to Public Policy', Institute of Economic Affairs, London (unpublished).

———— & L. Cromwell (1984), *Mutual Aid or Welfare State: Australia's Friendly Societies*, George Allen and Unwin, Sydney.

Gregory, R. (1992), 'Aspects of Australian Labour Force Living Standards: The Disappointing Decades 1970–90', paper presented to 21st Conference of Economists, University of Melbourne, July.

Hogbin Ercole & Associates & Logan Consulting (1991), 'Government Assistance for the Centre-based Child Care Industry in N.S.W.', report prepared for The Association of Child Care Centres of NSW, June.

Horton, P. & L. Alexander (1986), 'Freedom of Contract and the Family: A Skeptical Appraisal', pp.229–55 in J. Peden & F. Glahe (eds), *The American Family and the State*, Pacific Research Institute for Public Policy, San Francisco.

Institute of Public Affairs (1987), *Facts*, Melbourne, June-August.

Jones, A. (1988), 'Child Care Policy: Where to now?', *Current Affairs Bulletin*, November: 4–9.

Jordan, A. (1987), *The Common Treasury: The Distribution of Income to Families and Households*, AGPS, Canberra (Social Security Review).

Knox, T. (1945), *Hegel's Philosophy of Right*, Clarendon Press, Oxford.

Maley, B. (1990), 'Failing Families, Vanishing Australians, and the Welfare State', *Policy* 6(2): 17–21.

McDonald, P. (1983), 'Can the Family Survive?', *Australian Society*, 2 (11), 3–8.

———— (1988), paper presented for the Institute of Family Studies to a seminar on 'Social Welfare and Family Chaos', Australian Institute of Public Policy, Perth.

McGavin, P. (1992), *Wages and Welfare: The Failing Symbiosis*, Centre for Independent Studies, Sydney.

Mitchell, A. (1985), *Children in the Middle: Living Through Divorce*, Tavistock, London.

Morgan, P. (1989), 'Daddy Come Home', *The Spectator*, 2 September 2: 8–9.

Mount, F. (1982), *The Subversive Family: An Alternative History of Love and Marriage*, Jonathan Cape, London.

Murray, C. (1986), 'No, welfare isn't really the problem', *The Public Interest* 84 (Summer): 3–11.

National Women's Consultative Council (1991), 'Employer Sponsored Child Care — An Issues Paper', prepared by Community Child Care, Victoria, September.

Nygh, The Honourable Justice Peter, (1992), 'Should The Full Court Offer More Guidance To Judges Sitting At First Instance?', Fifth National Family Law Conference, Business Law Education Centre: 495–525.

Organisation for Economic Co-operation and Development (OECD) (1992), 'What is Household Non-market Production Worth?', *OECD Economic Studies* No. 18.

Pollard, A. (1991), 'The Family and the Economy', paper presented to Conference of the Australian Family Association.

Rawls, J. (1971), *A Theory of Justice*, Harvard University Press, Cambridge.

Rosenberg, N. & L. Birdzell, Jr. (1986), *How the West Grew Rich*, Basic Books, New York.

Sloan, J. (1992), *Australian Financial Review*, 6 July.

Spencer, I. (1992), 'Teenage Pregnancies and the Relationship to Long Term Unemployment', personal communication, February.

Swan, P. & M. Bernstam (1987), 'The Political Economy of the Interaction between Labour Market Regulation and the Social Welfare System', paper presented at *Australian Graduate School of Management One Day Conference:' Is the Australian Labour Market Ripe for Deregulation?'*, Sydney, July 8, 1–21.

———— (1989), 'Support for Single Parents', pp. 223–36 in M. James (ed.), *The Welfare State: Foundations and Alternatives*, Centre for Independent Studies, Sydney.

The Sydney Morning Herald (1991a), 'De Facto Couples Now the Norm', 26 December.

The Sydney Morning Herald (1991b), 'Matrimony: Our Million Dollar Divorce Debacle', 7 December.

Tapper, A. (1990a), *The Family in the Welfare State*, Allen and Unwin, Sydney, and Australian Institute for Public Policy, Perth.

———— (1990b), 'Taxing Families', *Quadrant* 34 (12): 43–6.

———— (1991), 'Who's really left carrying the baby?', *The Australian*, 2 January.

Teal, F. (1990), 'The Use and Cost of Child Care in Australia', Discussion Papers, Centre for Economic Policy Research, The Australian National University, Canberra.

Trainor, B. (1992), 'Why Australia's Divorce Law Should Be Reformed', *Policy* 8(1): 26–9.

Wallerstein, J. & J. Berlin Kelly (1980), *Surviving the Break-up: How Children and Parents Cope with Divorce*, Grant McIntyre, London.

Wallerstein, J. & S. Blakeslee (1989), *Second Chances: Men, Women and Children a Decade after Divorce*, Ticknor and Fields, New York.

Walsh, P. (1992), 'Document is child's play', *Australian Financial Review*, 25 August.

West, E. (1991a), 'The Rise of the State in Education. Part One: The Intellectual Background', *Policy* 7(1): 55–7.

—— (1991b). 'The Rise of the State in Education. Part Two: The Abolition of Parental Fees', *Policy* 7(2): 59–63.

Willetts, D. (1991), *Happy Families?: four points to a Conservative family policy*, Centre for Policy Studies, London.

Zinsmeister, K. (1988), 'Is Day Care Ruining Our Children?', *The Washington Post*, 25 September.

—— (1992), 'Parental Responsibility and the Future of the American Family', *Cornell Law Review* 77(5): 1001–7.

Index

Barry Maley